FUCK,
THAT'S
Delicious

This book is dedicated
to my grandmother, my
nonna, Alije Arslani.

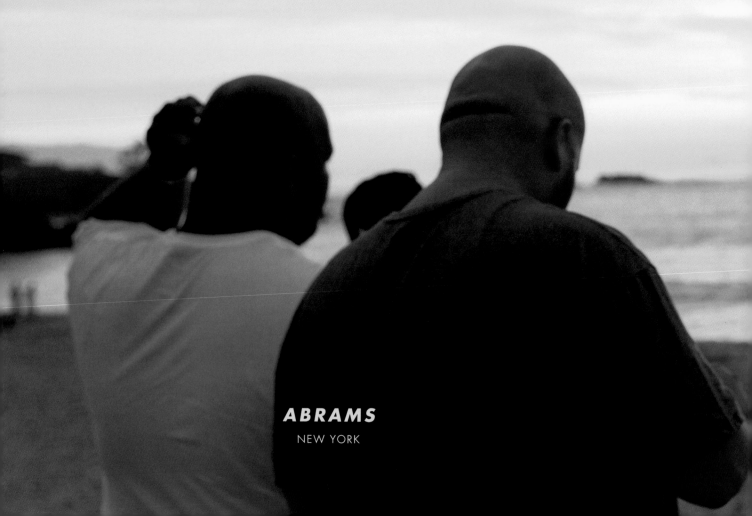

An Annotated Guide to
Eating Well by

ACTION BRONSON

with **RACHEL WHARTON**

ABRAMS

NEW YORK

FUCK,

THAT'S

Delicious

CONTENTS

My list of one hundred amazing things—the moments that got to me, the meals I ate, the places, the people, the artifacts, and the accessories.

SANDWICHES

Magical Doughs from the Balkans

PASTA

SPECIAL SAUCES

FRIED CHICKEN TEN DIFFERENT WAYS

Bebidas

ACTION BRONSON: THE NAME SOUNDS LIKE A VIDEO GAME, LIKE A DANCERSIZE CLASS, LIKE A '70S COP ACTION FLICK HELL-BENT ON JUSTICE AND REVENGE.

The dude looks like a wild cross between Godzilla, a handsome 1950s movie star from Europe, and a cult Mexican wrestler. On the surface, he looks extremely dangerous . . .

Bronsolino and I became instant friends the moment we met in La Piazza at Eataly in 2014 to tape a piece for his show—the title of which appears on the front cover of the book in your hot hands right now.

I had heard about AB through my kids who loved his mix tapes, his records, his persona, and his show, *FTD*, but we had never really crossed paths. What intrigued me first in the man himself were three things: his immense politeness, his relaxed and comfortable cadence when speaking about both music and food, and—above all—his intense curiosity. We have subsequently spoken for hours and hours and days and days about the pleasures and sensations of cooking and eating the things we love, the things we want to know about, and even the things that simply aren't our jams. His? Mackerel. Mine? Durian.

We have travelled widely together . . . to Don Peppe's in Ozone Park for scungilli and veal parm; to the eternal city of Roma, tasting everything from *trapizzino* and gelato to *cacio e pepe* and *la pajata*; to Sweden for fire-cooked deliciousness; and to Paris for three-star Michelin meals, both wearing long pants! Our appreciation for each other's whimsy, depth of knowledge, and thirst for more unites us as both creators and obsessive fans of the culinary arts and everything that can be, might be, and simply is fucking delicious.

We are *fratelli culinaria*, kitchen brothers on a thousand levels.

This book is a map of the inside of Bronson's brain. Starting with his version of Proust's madeleine, the "bagel with cheese," and then travelling down the THC-intensified paths of desire to include cheap street foods in the five boroughs of NYC to exotica found on his pilgrimages across the planet for the Munchies shows. We find every single thing that—like a shiny flash in a stream for a trout—draws us to eat, to make us happy, to fill us with joy and satisfaction. From charred broccoli to *döner* kebabs, from *petla* to *kerlana*, this magnificent tome is filled with both the recognizable and the perplexing. And, best of all, I can make it at home and so can you. This is not a tricky book filled with equipment from the science lab, there is no sous vide, there are no immersion circulators. This is a book that is at once a testament to a wild palate, to a man with a gastronomic vision, to a hip-hop artist of the top of the top category, and a student of life with legendary curiosity. Bronson is the Leonardo da Vinci of pop culture's multi-cosmic, infinitely overstimulated, twenty-first century children of the handheld devices. At the very same moment all this is swirling around in your head, on your tongue, throughout every single muscle of your dancing, jumping being, you realize . . . Fuck!!! This *is* delicious.

Cheers, my brother, and congrats.

This is one hell of a freshman thesis.
—Mario b

FOOD HAS BEEN A PART OF MY LIFE, ALWAYS.

I remember waking up to the smell of fresh bread as a youth, because my Albanian grandmother, my nonna, baked three times a day. My father's parents were originally from Kosovo, and for much of my childhood they lived with me and my parents at 69th Avenue and 164th Street in Flushing, Queens, in an area that is now called Fresh Meadows. They slept on the couch when they lived with us, in a small, two-bedroom apartment in a complex called Electchester, because it was built for the electricians' union. Sometimes my uncles, my aunts, and their kids—my cousins—lived there too. It was a hectic household at times. I remember my nonna and my aunts—everyone would be cooking together. My nonna was an incredible, incredible cook, baker, everything. Constantly making food, always had all these things prepared in the fridge, you'd just go and nosh. I guess she rubbed off on me. I don't know about Sunday dinner, because we had that every day, three meals a day. That's how we lived for years and years, until my grandparents went to my aunt's house in Brooklyn. Then my grandfather passed, and my nonna moved back to the Balkans—to Skopje, the capital of Macedonia, where they had first moved their family after they left Albania.

The part of Queens I grew up in was a crazy diverse area. Bagels, Jamaican food, Chinese food—I mean, it's New York. I would go over to my friends' houses, where it would be Indian, Spanish, Honduran food. You come over to my house, you eat Albanian. And my mother also took me out to places—to the city, to street fairs and flea markets, to Chinatown and Flushing with her Korean and Chinese friends, to good places in our neighborhood we would just go explore. My mom is the best—she exposed me to so much shit just being a free spirit herself.

Plus I always enjoyed being in the kitchen. When I was in junior high school, we actually still had a home ec type of class, where I met one of my good friends to this day, my man James, who you know as Meyhem Lauren. Our assignment was to make an egg. He had put about two inches worth of oil in the pan, and then he cracked the egg right into it. I was like, *What the fuck are you doing, man?* Now, that egg would be totally incredible: It's like a confit egg poached in oil. But he just didn't know what he was doing. He was just, *Yeah, I'm gonna make this*, laughing the whole time, doing it however he wanted. But from that point on, we were on. We would bring in steak, we would bring in things to make that we were totally not allowed to make, and we would just do it. I think that's where my love of cooking was first noticed by me. It's always been around me, but that's when I first applied it myself, I would say.

It was a long time from that to culinary school. I went through years of hanging out in the park, playing handball, being a man in New York City. Making my bones in the street, you know? I didn't really do great in high school, I was more of a fucking-around type of person. I played football for a little bit, but nothing could get through my head at the time, I was just doing whatever the fuck I wanted. I dropped out. I switched high schools. I went to a secondary school for kids who fuck up a lot. And I ended up graduating from a GED school: Went to class one time, the teacher told me not to come back until the test. I came back, took the test—I got like a 100 on it, I guess—and I got my diploma and went to culinary school at the Art Institute of New York in Manhattan down on Canal Street.

This was before *Top Chef*, before culinary schools were well-known—my mother did the research and found the school for me. My father had owned a restaurant for years and years and years, since I was six, and so I had

grown up in a professional kitchen type of atmosphere—like blue-collar people kind of kitchen. My mother, who is an amazing baker, made the desserts, and I would always go hang out there and fuck around with the chef, Rigoberto from Ecuador. He would take me in the back and show me how to do shit. Rigoberto was the first chef who actually showed me love in the kitchen, that it could be a good time. Seeing him in the kitchen made me want to be there. When I was eight or nine, I would go in the restaurant and ask him to make me food, and he would call me a little fat fuck. *Gordito!* With love, of course. I also remember him sprinkling parsley on top of the plate and calling it *poco de marihuana*, "a little bit of marijuana," you know. As a young kid, my mind was blown.

So after I got that GED I just thought, *Fuck it, I'll go through with culinary school, let's go.* I got the loan—I just finished paying it off recently, in fact—and I went. I liked culinary school a lot because I was doing well, I was excelling. I already knew a lot of shit, and so girls especially would look to me for help. That school was where everything popped off. I was meeting a lot of new people, and I was in the city for the first time. I never went to school in Manhattan before. It was good, going downtown every day. It's good to do that when you're young, to walk around the city and get a feel for who and where and what you are. But as I was about to get ready to complete my last year, I was also about to have my first child. I needed a job, so I left school and started working for my father. It was only two people in the kitchen, and I was one of them. Years passed, six or seven. I was cooking, purchasing for the place, smoking weed. I was a fuckhead, I admit. I would leave the restaurant whenever I wanted, I would come in whenever, 'cause we all knew my father's schedule. I would be sneaky. I wasn't taking it seriously, and I wasn't taking things seriously.*

I wanted to explore new things, and I starting working for the Mets at Citi Field. I played baseball my entire life, so this was sick, working in the ballpark, walking through the tunnel. The clubhouse was right next door to my kitchen, I

---

* I used to have to open the restaurant early for brunch, but I didn't have a key. I had to climb through the window of the fucking restaurant to get in every morning. So one day this lady is just jogging by, and I'm breaking into the restaurant to go work, and she starts screaming at the top of her lungs that she's going to call the cops. A whole thing ensues, I start cursing her out, retaliating with a war of words. Later, I flip out on my father. Bottom line, on Yelp she wrote a massive paragraph about how she saw the chef breaking into the restaurant.

could see the guys coming in, you know. You would give them high fives and shit, and some dudes would occasionally come into the kitchen. It was just ill to be in that atmosphere, before the games, through the games with thousands of people around, and after the games when everyone but us and the players had left. I loved all of it.

That was a good job for a while, a few years. I was excelling there as well. But my temper got the best of me one day and just pushed me over the edge. I got into a confrontation, and I hurt somebody, and just as that happened all the heads of the ballpark—the GMs of each department—were doing their rounds. I was fired right on the spot. The head chef tried to get me my job back—I was seasonal at the time, there just for the games, working toward getting full time. Didn't happen: It wasn't made for me to be a chef for the Mets, you know what I mean?

So I go back to my father's spot for a minute, and I break my leg within a week of being back full time. January 31, 2011. It changed my life, right there.

I wasn't really making music for real yet, right then. I took it on in 2008 as a little hobby. But you know, hobbies get crazy. Eventually I just became infatuated, writing raps, going to the studio when I could afford to. It first started when my old home ec friend Meyhem Lauren was making an album. I was going to his sessions, and my boy was just, *Yo, why don't you write something to get on the album?* And I ended up doing something—I rapped. And I was like, *Here we go. Might as well. I've been around it my entire life, why the fuck not?* So I was on my first mixtape.

Then there was a video posted of me rapping in 2009, a plain black and white video of me doing a song called "A Come Up Freestyle." I didn't even know you could put music on the Internet besides Napster or LimeWire. I hadn't had the Internet in ten years, not since AOL dialup. Somebody else had put it up on Myspace, and they were cool with some dude who runs a hip-hop blog called OnSmash, which posted it. And it got thirty thousand views. *What the fuck, thirty thousand people saw this?* (Now you don't even think ten million's enough. You're like, *I need more! Fifty million, a hundred million.*)

When I broke my leg, there was no money being made at all for my music, no thought of money. I was living with my mother. Since I couldn't work in a kitchen, I was just working,

Vice crew in Italy. Me and Meyhem, Jack, Bernardo, Tom, plus some dudes from Vice Italy.

working, working on my music, just for myself for a long time. I liked it without anybody around me or with me. Just doing what I wanted, my own thing. Even before I broke my leg, there would be times when I asked my mother for money to go to the studio, because I was making shitty money then. She would always support me with whatever she had. Always. She wasn't making lots of money either, but she'd give me enough money to go to the studio for two hours, to put my songs and my mixtapes out myself before I got signed to a label. My mother started my shit off.

Then, while I was still in my sickbed, somebody from overseas paid me to do a verse. Then I got about four more of those little gigs—until I had $2,000 saved up. I went out and got more work, until it became $10,000 that I had in my hand. Alright, I thought, this is the base for something. I put out the first of many self-made projects, called *Bon Appetit . . . . . Bitch!!!!!* And the fucking ball just rolled from there.

I started doing shows. Killing at shows, really making my bones as a performer doing shows. I have a crazy live show, and so people kept coming back. In London, everywhere in Europe, it just evolved into something else. And I think who I was helped a lot. I am still a regular guy: A normal dude from Queens who went to work every day. I just somehow have a knack for certain things while other people might have a knack for other things. I rap about what I know, what I fucking love.

Before I broke my leg, before I was really rapping, I'd already made some cooking videos. Simple stuff. How to cut an onion. The Bronson burger. Spaghetti and shrimp. And my whole life, me and Meyhem and Big Body Bes— who I say is my cousin, because he's also Albanian— would always go out to eat, find places to eat. That's our favorite pastime—it's just what we did. And so when I went on tour with Eminem for *Blue Chips 2*, I had a good friend of mine, Tom Gould, a videographer I've done a lot of work with, come with me. We went to New Zealand, South Africa, London, and Australia so we could make the first episodes of what would become my Viceland show *Fuck, That's Delicious*. We brought it to Chris Grosso, the executive producer of *Munchies* at Vice, and he made it a reality. We actually called it *Adventure Time with Action Bronson* at first, but then as I was rubbing a bit of fake coke on my mouth in a Chinese restaurant in my video for "The Symbol," I looked up and said, *Fuck, that's delicious.*

That's where the name of the show came from. It is literally a feeling. There are no other words to describe what you just ate. You just have to curse and be vulgar and violent, you know what I mean?

This book captures all those moments, all those foods that got to me, all the things that you should try also. When Momma makes me a good ol' bagel and cheese with scrambled eggs—the eggs gotta be very softly scrambled—or she makes me a traditional Albanian dish called *pite*, which is a dough filled with cheese my grandmother taught her to make. The malted at Eddie's Sweet Shop, which has been a Queens staple for years— everybody knows about that spot if they're from the area. The tacos at Maxwell Street Market in Chicago, foraging with a dude named Yoda in Perth, Dominican *chimis*. Real Jamaican jerk. Hand-rolled pasta from Mario Batali and Michael White, my heroes. Smoked lamb, red pepper, and onion stew in Turkish pita in the back of a Danish metal bar, or a family meal at one of the best restaurants in the world. The best Chinese red pork buns in the world, found in London, or hanging out with chefs I used to watch on TV at home in my underwear.

This book is all things I like, all things I got to taste and try over the past few years, many with Meyhem, Body, and my deejay The Alchemist. They are all part of the TV show now, and you'll see them throughout this book too. We've eaten some truly fucking delicious meals, so many sometimes I have to look at Instagram to refresh my memory. Somehow I left my job as a chef and made it back into the world of food through my music. That's the world I wanted to be in from the beginning. I go around the world to perform for people, and I am able to see the most incredible places, taste the most incredible things, while still getting paid. Last year, I was diving for clams in Western Australia in some unknown waters, an hour hike from anywhere. It was a wild place—the farthest place from New York that you could possibly be. I came up out of the water and I saw a camera in my face, and I had an epiphany. I come from Queens—my life is crazy at this point, you know? But it just felt right, like the universe was telling me that this was my calling.

I couldn't think of a better job. Rap does a lot of wonderful things. The show, this book, my life, is definitely something I've been wanting to do for a very, very, very long time, and I'm just happy that it's come to life. ●

A BOWL OF CRISPIX OVER THE SINK

1.

I've been standing over the kitchen sink at my mother's house eating Crispix for thirty years, out of a bowl with a fat Italian chef on it. (I also must have a small spoon— I can't eat cereal with a big spoon.) This is stoner food for me—if I buy a box of Crispix, it's over. I just scarf it down in one sitting. It's been breakfast, lunch, and dinner, everything. Both Crispix and Rice Krispies are 100 percent lifers, as in I will love them for life. There are other cereals when I go on binges: Product 19, which was an old-people cereal I loved, and Lucky Charms, but only the marshmallows. Each cereal has its own special way of being eaten: Crispix and Rice Krispies are always served with skim milk. Cookie Crisp, Cinnamon Toast Crunch, and Fruity Pebbles, these get no milk—these you just drink out of the box. Rice Krispies must be eaten almost like a risotto, meaning you put enough milk in there to where you can stir it but it's still kind of crunchy. None of them beat Crispix, the best cereal ever invented.

19

2. CHANKONABE

In Japan it is a very, very rare thing for foreigners to be invited into the stable where sumo wrestlers live and work,* much less step out into the circle. The wrestlers' lives are consumed by sumo; after they take the vow, they are sumo. They live together, eat every meal together, and when they make a public appearance, they go wrapped in the traditional warrior clothing—it looks like a kilt but is much cooler—so everybody knows what they are. It's an ancient life. When we were in Tokyo filming *Fuck, That's Delicious*, they let us train a little bit in the ring, and then they made this traditional stew called *chankonabe*, or sumo stew. With chankonabe, everybody sits around this big pot filled with a soy and sesame soup base. They add some chicken, then let that cook for awhile; then they add bok choy and vegetables. The sumo serve it with very thinly sliced pork cooked with onions—almost like a Philly cheesesteak with no cheese. You put a little mayo on the side of the steak, and then you stir it all together a little at a time. The grandmaster leading the meal was an *ozeki*, meaning he's one of the grand champions of sumo. Because he isn't Japanese born—he's Samoan, from Hawaii—he can't be *yokozuna*, which is the title given to the highest grand champion from Japan. But ozeki is right under yokozuna, so he's still considered a huge star. And let me tell you something—people go to Japan and talk about ramen this, that, the other. I think the chankonabe was by far the best soup I ever had. When I tell you those sumo motherfuckers put their foot in it, I mean it was better than any broth ever in the history of life. I didn't expect it to be that good. I never even had ramen on that trip to Japan because I didn't want to ruin my chankonabe situation.

✱ I also got to see extreme wrestling in Japan, the death matches with piranha tanks and barbed wire and shit like that. I want you to look up Big Japan Pro Wrestling and check that out when you get a chance. It's next level.

In Japan, clockwise from top left: At Les Créations de Narisawa in Tokyo. At a street festival in Shibuya where we carried saints on our backs. Eating cotton candy on Harajuku Street, Shibuya Crossing.

3. BAGEL WITH CHEESE

Now we're going to get deep. For me, love has always been shown with a bagel. If I did something good as a kid, I got a bagel. If I was hungry, I got a bagel. And if I was upset? *Get the fucking kid a bagel.* I remember waking up almost every day to the smell of coffee and toasting sesame bagels, like a dream. When I was really young, I wouldn't try any of the different ethnic foods my Albanian nonna would make. She and my grandfather lived with us for years, and she was always cooking. There was so much great shit around in our kitchen to eat—dried chickpeas for snacking, this white bean stew called *pasul*, homemade bread of all kinds—but until I got a little older, I wouldn't try any of it. Instead my mother, and then my nonna too, would always make me a toasted bagel with cheese. They would scoop out the dough from the inside of the bagel—sesame or maybe a plain, but nothing else—fill the hole with Polly-O whole milk mozzarella cheese, and then run it under the broiler until it was just the way I liked it: The cheese had to be nice and bubbly and browned and the bagel crispy, its edges toasted a deep dark brown.

In the summers, when my cousins and I were home from school, we got a bag of bagels early in the morning before we went to the beach.* We'd hit the bagel store near our house and order a couple with sliced American cheese and turkey or roast beef and maybe a little mustard, or sometimes with just a slice of mozzarella to mimic the bagel with cheese I usually ate at home. Later I would come out of the water and I would eat a bagel sandwich sitting in the shade under the umbrella on a blanket with my mother. I haven't been to Jones Beach in a long time, but being there every summer is a deep memory that I have, and bagels trigger it for me.

---

* Robert Moses State Park almost always, or if we got out early enough, Jones Beach Field Six—it had the shortest walk from the parking lot—or Rockaway Park in Queens.

Bagels were also there when my mother and I would visit my grandparents in West Palm Beach, as we did often. My grandmother was already in a nursing home there in Florida—she had Alzheimer's for as long as I could remember her—and my grandfather and my mother and I would stop in almost every morning to get a bagel on the way to see her, which we did every single day we were there. My grandfather loved to take us to restaurants, and in Florida the bagel shops weren't the little deli-like things they are in New York City—they're more like diners. So our day started with breakfast together at the bagel shop. My grandfather would get grits, my mother would get poached eggs, and I would get soft scrambled eggs and a toasted bagel. Those trips out to get bagels in the morning were always a highlight for my mother and her father, and now they're a highlight for me and my mom.

I still believe a bagel is the perfect food, and a bagel with cheese prepared as my mother and I make it is one of the best things on earth. It's something that I now make for myself often. It is just the right combination and contrast—almost burnt, crunchy caramelized ends up against the soft doughiness of the interior, and then finally the creamy saltiness of the cheese, which just sends everything over the edge. It's a perfect bite—every single food group I need in my life. Everybody has the thing that gives them comfort and satisfaction no matter how many times they eat it, and the bagel with cheese is mine. Many of my friends are now addicted to these bagels: They love the goddamn bagel with cheese. To me, it's just like a perfect hit of THC—it's a fifteen-minute orgasm of straight bagel bliss. I don't think that there's anything else that makes me happier, period. I know it's terrible for me, but what am I going to do? They'll eventually kill me one day, but I guess I'll die happy.

ANATOMY OF A BAGEL WITH CHEESE

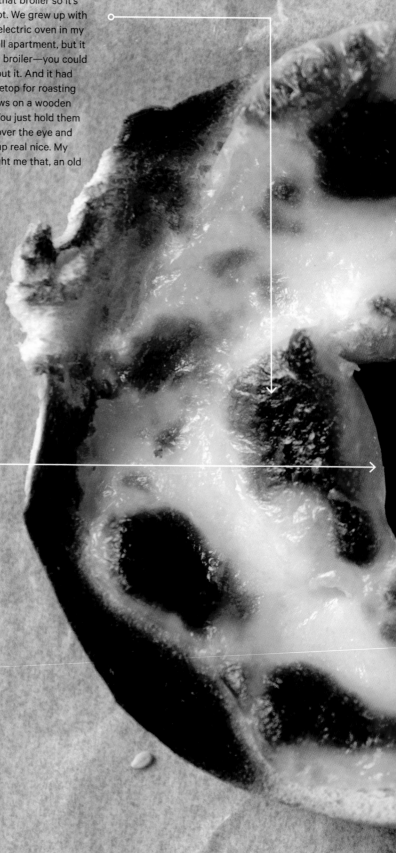

1. Preheat that broiler so it's good and hot. We grew up with just a plain electric oven in my family's small apartment, but it had an even broiler—you could say that about it. And it had a great stovetop for roasting marshmallows on a wooden chopstick. You just hold them right there over the eye and they sizzle up real nice. My mother taught me that, an old family trick.

2. Use only a sesame seed bagel, or, if you must, plain. Toasted sesame seeds really add something to this bagel—plus sesame is one of my favorite flavors in life. I keep a bag of plain or sesame bagels from Utopia Bagels in Queens in my freezer at all times and defrost them when I need them. (You do just 30 seconds in the microwave, you feel me? Otherwise the bagel gets hard.) An egg bagel, an everything bagel—I can get behind those, but a sesame bagel, there's nothing like it. I have had breakfast all over Europe, and they have these traditional breads that are round, and they have sesame seeds all over them, and it's doughy in the center. It's a bagel or something very similar, but they don't call it a bagel, they call it a *gevrek* or a *koulouri* or a *simit*. I believe making dough into a circular shape and baking it with some kind of seed in it probably has been done since the beginning of time.

3. One of the things I like about the bagel more so than other breads is that inside crevice—note that it's not a totally round hole. It is usually kind of stuck together in places, so that when you toast it you get a nice doughiness where it comes together but a crispy edge where it's separated. Not a step, per se, but important nonetheless.

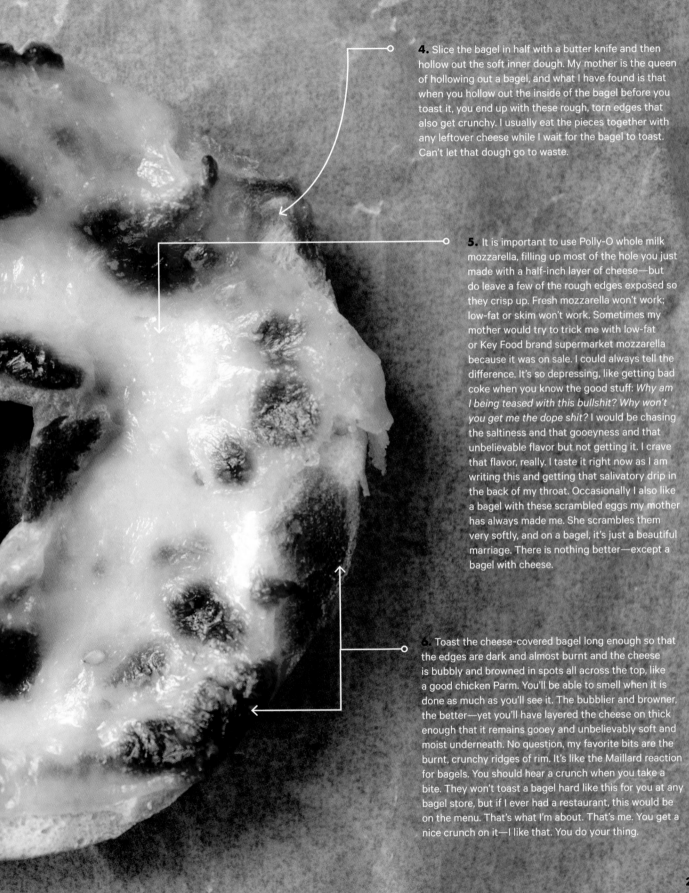

4. Slice the bagel in half with a butter knife and then hollow out the soft inner dough. My mother is the queen of hollowing out a bagel, and what I have found is that when you hollow out the inside of the bagel before you toast it, you end up with these rough, torn edges that also get crunchy. I usually eat the pieces together with any leftover cheese while I wait for the bagel to toast. Can't let that dough go to waste.

5. It is important to use Polly-O whole milk mozzarella, filling up most of the hole you just made with a half-inch layer of cheese—but do leave a few of the rough edges exposed so they crisp up. Fresh mozzarella won't work; low-fat or skim won't work. Sometimes my mother would try to trick me with low-fat or Key Food brand supermarket mozzarella because it was on sale. I could always tell the difference. It's so depressing, like getting bad coke when you know the good stuff: *Why am I being teased with this bullshit? Why won't you get me the dope shit?* I would be chasing the saltiness and that gooeyness and that unbelievable flavor but not getting it. I crave that flavor, really. I taste it right now as I am writing this and getting that salivatory drip in the back of my throat. Occasionally I also like a bagel with these scrambled eggs my mother has always made me. She scrambles them very softly, and on a bagel, it's just a beautiful marriage. There is nothing better—except a bagel with cheese.

6. Toast the cheese-covered bagel long enough so that the edges are dark and almost burnt and the cheese is bubbly and browned in spots all across the top, like a good chicken Parm. You'll be able to smell when it is done as much as you'll see it. The bubblier and browner, the better—yet you'll have layered the cheese on thick enough that it remains gooey and unbelievably soft and moist underneath. No question, my favorite bits are the burnt, crunchy ridges of rim. It's like the Maillard reaction for bagels. You should hear a crunch when you take a bite. They won't toast a bagel hard like this for you at any bagel store, but if I ever had a restaurant, this would be on the menu. That's what I'm about. That's me. You get a nice crunch on it—I like that. You do your thing.

FIVE BAGELS AROUND THE WORLD.

No matter where I am, I'm always drawn to bagels, as I am under their spell. Each year I continue my journey of trying to figure out who does the better bagel. But perhaps that doesn't matter—perhaps I should just enjoy the whimsical enchantment of each. Either way, here are five special bagels in my life.

UTOPIA BAGELS: FLUSHING, QUEENS

The best bagel in New York City used to be from Bagel Oasis,* a twenty-four-hour place on Horace Harding Expressway not far from where I grew up in Flushing, Queens. I was raised on these bagels, and people come from all over the place to get them—as they've been doing since 1961. Then I found Utopia Bagels on Utopia Parkway. They hand roll, slow proof, boil-then-bake—these bagels take thirty-six hours to make and are chewy, dense. Utopia Bagels has been going since 1981, but it just doubled in size right before I went the first time. These bagels are fire—the very best in the city, in my opinion. Now I usually have a bag in my freezer, even though I also go there all the time when I am home. In addition to my standard sesame or plain bagel with cheese, I've come up with another Utopia Bagels concoction that I really like: A toasted cinnamon raisin bagel with jalapeño cream cheese.

 There was also Bagels Plus, which was just up the block on Parsons Boulevard. We'd go there sometimes on the way to the beach, but it's so close to home you really can't go in there without bumping into some schmuck you know that you don't want to see at nine in the morning, stuck in a fake conversation about the weather. Whenever people are uncomfortable, they talk about the weather. Or the Yankees. But weather is more universal—plus there's always something to talk about: It's nature's soap opera.

BAGEL LAND/ BAGEL WORLD: WEST PALM BEACH, FLORIDA

In West Palm Beach, where my mother's parents lived when I was in grade school, I remember we either went to Bagel Land or Bagel World.* I forget which one was better, but this was the routine every single day: My grandfather would take me and my mother to one of the two bagel shops for breakfast, and then we would watch a few VHS tapes, a great collection of which I still have in a cabinet behind the couch at my mother's house in Queens. Then we would go to the nursing home to see my grandmother, who had Alzheimer's, and we would sit there with her for most of the day before my grandfather took us out to dinner. Food was always love to him. His name was Irving Lovett, and he came to the United States on a boat from Russia to Ellis Island. He spoke Yiddish and he also had a strong New York accent, very old-timey. He was a great dude, a big guy with a beautiful head of white hair and a big personality, and he would make everybody in the room laugh. He was always a little inappropriate, in a very Rodney Dangerfield way. He is missed.

 At least I remember them as Bagel Land and Bagel World. My mother, who was older and paying more attention, says at least one of them was called New York Bagel.

LA MAISON: MONTREAL, CANADA

When in Montreal, this is the bagel spot to go to. The last time I went there I didn't even have anything on mine—I just ate half a dozen sesame by myself sitting right there in front of the store. They were so majestically warm, just out of the wood-burning oven, that when I broke them open I should have been wearing asbestos gloves. A New York bagel is nothing like a Montreal bagel. They say it's the water—it's more than that. It's a whole other system of making them that gives them that special exterior crunch, that makes them that dense. It's just a whole different thing.

BEIGEL BAKE: LONDON, ENGLAND

I usually do two things as soon as I land in London: Go to Lahore Kebab House (see page 125) for lamb chops and go get a bagel from Beigel Bake, which is not too far around the corner down on Brick Lane, an old Londontown street lined with little shops and Indian curry restaurants.* I love Brick Lane, and Beigel Bake has been kicking it there since 1974. Their bagels are smaller, more like a Lender's than a typical modern New York City bagel—yeasty, chewy, and a little crispy on the outside. Beigel Bake is open twenty-four hours, but their bagels are always fresh because this place pumps them out like crazy all day long. It is always packed. There are always junkies out front, and the women who run it are always mean, in a good way. You can get your bagel with lox or boiled chicken or butter and a thick slice of cheap British salami, plus a bunch of other things, but the main objective at Beigel Bake has always been the salt beef—big slabs of this salty, stringy meat barely stuffed inside that soft little bagel. It is the only filling they add to order—the rest are already made and ready to go in plastic buckets. It is also just a little too salty to eat straight up like pastrami or corned beef, but somehow with that strong sharp English mustard they have and that bagel, it works.

✱ I've been told that there's better Indian food in London than there is in India, and Manchester is a fucking close second: Curry Mile in Manchester is nothing to be fucked with. It is literally a mile of curry restaurants, nonstop, back and forth.

BEST UGLY BAGELS: AUCKLAND, NEW ZEALAND

Best Ugly Bagels is a bagel factory owned by Chef Al Brown, the man who is also responsible for making what I believe is the best smoked meat that I have ever tasted (see page 94). His bagel shop is called Best Ugly because the bagels are cooked next to a wood fire and prone to inconsistencies, so it's an inside joke about their appearance: *I'm unique in my own way; I am beautiful on the inside.* That's good, because when I got to make one myself on my last trip to New Zealand, I had just broken my hand.* Uglys are mainly Montreal-style bagels, which means made with honey and without salt, a little bit different from the bagels I am used to, but still absolutely sublime. Like the best soft pretzel you ever tasted. Al's standard Ugly is topped with sesame seeds, and you already know anything sesame toasted is all me. Al's bagel factory is also just sick—he uses an Old World technique, the same style used in Montreal, where he worked as a chef for a few years. The bagels are cooked on long wooden paddles in this unbelievable wood-burning contraption that runs on the same New Zealand mānuka wood he uses to smoke his meats. These bagels are fussed over: They're taken out and flipped over about halfway through, so that the flat bottom found on most bagels doesn't form. This one is round all around—all top, all crunch, no flat surface. When they're fully done, you slide the paddle out from the oven and flip it into the air in one quick motion, and the bagels all come falling down right into the basket where they need to be. It's a beautiful thing.

✱ The computer kept fucking up, and it was just throwing off my entire chi. When you perform, you need a certain vibe, you need a certain energy. I went backstage in a blind rage, saw something that I thought I could probably break through, I punched it, I didn't break through it, and instead broke my hand. And then I had to come back out on stage and rap the rest of the show with my hand in a bucket of ice.

USDA FOOD PYRAMID

GOLDEN BEET POKE

I'm a beet bitch: I love beets.

They have a sweet, earthy, rustic type of emotion. Ask Mario. It's what I always order at his restaurant Babbo—that and the octopus and five kinds of pasta. All root vegetables, really, are amazing. A few years ago, when I went to the Banzai Pipeline on the island of Oahu to do a show at the Pipe Masters surfing competition, I came home dreaming of poke. It's a Hawaiian thing, this delicious shit you just go get at the corner store in Hawaii, with chips and Gatorade, made of cut-up chunks of raw fish usually dressed with soy sauce and green onions, but you can go from there. I was shopping at the farmers' market the first time I ever tried to make it at home, high out of my mind, and I spotted some golden beets. I poke-ed that too, and invented some delicious shit.

GOLDEN BEET POKE

This dish looks fucking good,
like the cover of *Bon Appétit*.

SERVES 2

You know the Hawaiian chef dude who always does the luaus on TV, Roy Yamaguchi? He's the one who first put me on to this shit. But now poke is trendy—anything healthy is trendy. At the Kahuku Superette on the Kamehameha Highway in Hawaii, they serve their special poke bowls in plastic takeout containers over a pile of white rice and you eat it with wooden chopsticks, the kind you get with Chinese takeout.

1-inch piece (22 g) fresh ginger, peeled
2 green onions, trimmed and thinly sliced
½ Maui, Vidalia, or other large sweet onion,
    quartered and thinly sliced
2 cups (280 g) peeled, roasted golden beets cut into
    ¾-inch (2 cm) cubes (See **NOTE**)
2–3 tablespoons soy sauce
1 tablespoon sesame oil
1 tablespoon cane sugar
1 tablespoon chopped medium-hot fresh chile,
    such as jalapeño
1 tablespoon sesame seeds, freshly toasted,
    plus extra for garnish
3 tablespoons chopped fresh cilantro leaves,
    for garnish
½ tablespoon Japanese togarashi spice mix,
    or to taste
Fresh limes
Steamed white rice

1. Grate the ginger into a large mixing bowl. You want about 1½ tablespoons. If you don't have a grater, just start spooning it—scraping the ginger into the bowl. It's like juicing it at the same time. Then add the onions.

2. Toss the beets into the bowl and add 2 tablespoons of the soy sauce, and the sesame oil, cane sugar, and chopped chile.

3. Give it all a nice toss, a nice mix-up, then taste. Let it sit in the icebox a little bit until it's chilled. (The icebox is the refrigerator.)

4. Hit it with the toasted sesame seeds, which changes the whole complexity of the dish, right there. I like to use white and black, aka the swirl.

5. Get some good cilantro from the farmers' market. Now you're going to hit it with that. Sprinkle the bowl with togarashi, then you hit it with some lime juice to liven it up.

6. Adjust the seasoning to your liking, adding more soy, sugar, togarashi, and lime juice as you like, sprinkle on a few more sesame seeds, and serve over white rice.

NOTE: From about 1 pound (455 g) of beets. I know people usually don't put olive oil on their beets when they roast them whole, but I think they get really dry otherwise. I drizzle it on and let them soak it up on the pan so as they roast it gets sticky and shit, about an hour at 400°F (205°C). Let them cool and you can just peel them with your hands. That's why we roast golden beets; they don't stain the hands.

5. FRIED POTATOISH SITUATIONS

A French fry is always a magical thing: Belgian-style, the shoestrings, steak fries like they do at an old diner, crinkle cuts, and the waffle, which is so underutilized. The Israeli fries, they're great as well—they're softly cooked at a low temperature to be a little mushier and perfect on the falafel sandwich. I also learned to make real French fries from the same guy that taught me My Special Sauce (page 189). You fry them three times, and you use duck fat every time. The first time is light: You fry at 200 to 250°F (90 to 120°C), then take 'em out, let 'em sit for a bit. The second fry is fast, at 275 to 300°F (135 to 150°C), and then you let them chill in the fridge. The last fry is at 350 to 360°F (177 to 182°C). You throw 'em in there cold, and they're going to turn out almost like airy mashed potatoes inside of a crispy fry. Next level.

I also have a two-fry vegetable oil method I learned from my man Jusaid, a Mexican who worked at my father's restaurant: The first cook is at a low temperature to soften them, then you throw them into the freezer or the fridge before you fry them again at a higher temperature. Honestly, I probably could make French fries in at least five ways. Back in the day, I even went as far as to buy the Super Slicer and the mechanical potato peeler on QVC, the one where you stick it in the potato and it peels it in perfectly round circles. (Along with a whole bunch of college basketball cards and those little basketball hoops for the crib.)

But in other parts of the world you also have your *tostones* and *maduros*—which are plantains—and your fried yuca, which is cassava. The tostones and the fried yuca are savory, while the maduro is sweet. The sweet ones are where it's at, and the main thing about the maduros is that to make them, the plantain has to be totally disgusting-looking and black—that's when you're going to get the sweetest candy-tasting niblets that you've ever tasted in your life. I like to do them in a shallow pan with a little bit of oil and cook them slowly on either side, so they kind of absorb the oil and get soft all the way through, then turn up the heat to get a candy crunch on the outside. You don't need to add any sugar, because they have their own, but add a little salt to them and it's a beautiful thing.

Tostones are fried twice also, but those plantains have to be as unripe and as green as possible. The Caribbean people have this genius way of cooking a plantain—same technique as a French fry, once again. Once is like a quick fry, then you take them out and you mash them down with something—with the bottom of a pan, your hand, the bottom of a coffee cup—and then you put them back in the fryer and you get them fucking crunched like you can't believe. You can top these things with anything—with shrimp, with ceviche, guacamole, you can eat them as fries, you can slice them extra thin and eat them as chips. You can do the same thing with the sweet ones and make sweet chips dusted with a little salt.

And the yuca . . . I think I like it even better than a potato. It's a root and it's poisonous unless you cook it, but it's one of the most sought-after products in an African kitchen, an indigenous plant that's used for everything. You pound it, you dry it, you make flour with it, you fry it, you do this, you do that. I love it fried, but I've also been introduced to the Dominican style *yuca encebollada*, which is where you boil it very slowly or you steam it to where it is transparent and falls apart ever so gorgeously like silk, and then you hit it with some sort of oil and vinegar-ed red onion. Oof. I was told traditionally you eat that with *pollo guisado*, or stewed chicken.

POT PIE

Growing up, I had never had a potpie. I am from New York. Why would I have heard of a chicken potpie? Then I went to Boston Market after that first came out, and I had a chicken pot pie and it blew my mind how delicious it was. It was exciting shit: It was sagey, it tasted like Thanksgiving. It's all about the stew, but no, it's all about the crust. It's really about both together, perfectly. I don't ever remember seeing a potpie in my freezer section before that, and then out of nowhere, there it was—Marie Callender's. Over the years I have perfected the way to heat it up. You have to put aluminum foil around the brim of the pie so it doesn't go dark. It's just like baking any other pie, but not everyone knows that, and that's a good little trick. It comes out so unbelievable, with a crunchy dough, but you have to let it sit for a second before you eat it, to let it congeal. What I do is I break open the crust and let it just hang out halfway in the stew, kind of like a cookie with milk. You know how you get some crispy part but some soft part that slowly works its way up? It's like the way a tree sucks up all the juice from the roots. I am now a potpie whore. Recently I had a potpie at Gjusta in Los Angeles that was phenomenal, just a more refined, upscale version of Boston Market's, which really made me happy. It had that familiar taste that you expect in a potpie, and the crunch—it had just come out of the oven when they gave it to me, and it was the perfect symphony of stew and crust.

MEYHEM LAUREN'S CHICKEN PATTY POTPIE

You could also call this chicken curry en croute.

MAKES 2 10-INCH (25 CM) DEEP-DISH POTPIES

This is Meyhem's creation, and it started out as Thai chicken curry, but it really tastes like a big Jamaican chicken patty. Meyhem uses store-bought piecrusts in the shell (he cuts the edge off one and pops it upside down on the other) and usually makes a smaller pie, but I make my own crusts. You can use the Pillsbury fill-and-bake ones—with the lard, you just unroll them—but you'll want to baste them with extra butter. This is literally exactly as he made it.

1½–2 pounds (680-900 g) boneless chicken thighs
6 cloves garlic, smashed
Curry powder
Vegeta
Paprika
Olive oil
4 small carrots, peeled and diced
3 ribs celery, diced
1 red onion, diced
2 8-ounce boxes cremini mushrooms, stemmed and quartered
2 long red chiles sliced on the bias
2 cans light coconut milk
1 can pickled jalapeños

3 tablespoons lemon zest
1 thumb-size knob ginger, smashed and diced
1 small bunch basil, tough stems removed
3 small Idaho potatoes, cut into large dice
2 ripe tomatoes
1 tablespoon brown sugar
4 large piecrusts
1 stick softened butter
Flaky sea salt
1 egg, beaten

1. Preheat the oven to 425°F (220°C).

2. Combine the chicken and garlic in a large mixing bowl. Sprinkle the chicken on all sides with curry powder, Vegeta, paprika, and olive oil. Mix to coat and let sit for 15 to 20 minutes, then brown over medium heat on all sides in a Dutch oven. It should look yellow, like the halal truck chicken in Manhattan.

3. Remove the chicken to a plate and cook the vegetables (carrots, celery, onion, mushrooms, and chiles) in the same pot until they are soft, scraping up any brown bits from the chicken.

4. Add the chicken back to the pot, pour in the coconut milk and the pickled jalapeños, and bring everything to a simmer.

5. Add the lemon zest, ginger, basil, potatoes, and tomatoes, crushing the tomatoes with your hands into the pot and discarding the skins when you're done. Stir in the sugar. Taste for salt, sugar, heat, etc.

6. Simmer until potatoes are cooked through—at least 20 minutes—smashing them a bit as they cook with a wooden spoon to release their starches. Use the spoon to slightly shred the chicken. Let it cool down before adding it to the pie.

7. Meanwhile, grease two spring-form cake pans with lots of butter and sprinkle on some sea salt. Press in the crusts and chill in the refrigerator.

8. When the curry has cooled, place it in the cake pans with a slotted spoon so you don't add too much liquid. Add the top crusts. Crimp around the edges and make a few slits around each center point with a knife, like on a regular pie.

9. Bake until the filling is bubbling through the slits, then baste the tops with butter and the beaten egg at least once, if not twice, and continue to bake until really golden brown and the edges are dark brown and crunchy.

10. Serve with Crystal Hot Sauce.

7. A KEY FOOD BAG

The plastic grocery bags you carry home from the Key Food supermarket were my book bag, my ziplock bag, my school lunch box, my Louis Vuitton luggage. You just put your keys and wallet and whatever else you need in there, then tie it at the top and take it with you. The collection of Key Food bags my mother still has in her apartment is insane. Some hang on the side of one thing; more are tucked into another place. It is a hilarious collection of plastic baggages.

8. CHEWY CANDIES

My life at one point was about stealing Starburst,* wearing a fisherman's vest, and putting quarters up on the video games to make sure everybody knew I got next. I am serious: This was a couple decades ago, right across the street from my mother's house in Flushing at Larry's and Lill's, which was a candy store and a diner with games like *Mortal Kombat* and *NBA Jam*. My scheme was standing really close to the candy wearing this fisherman's vest and then sliding the candies into a long, skinny pocket. I had an issue with stealing anything that wasn't exactly the right size for the pocket. I took Now & Laters, the ones that come three to a pack, the longer Tootsie Rolls, the Starburst: They all fit perfectly flush. Plus, these were also my favorite types of candy—anything with that chewy texture I love, like Brach's caramels, Milk Duds, Raisinets, Fruit Gushers, Fruit Roll-Ups, and Fruit by the Foot. (A

Tootsie Roll is still my favorite candy, though Raisinets is an addiction I'm constantly trying to kick like heroin, and it *always* wins. It's OK, though, because there's a lot of antioxidants.)

By that point, Larry's and Lill's was owned by this Korean guy, Mr. Lee, who used to call me Onion. My real name is Ariyan, and he pronounced that *onion*, and I do kind of resemble an onion—a shallot, to be specific. Mr. Lee and his wife used to work at the store together, and they would just go at it, even though I felt like they were probably just talking about egg and cheese on a roll. Mr. Lee wasn't really a nice guy—he would yell at everybody. That's why we stole from him, I guess. Every morning the same crowd from the neighborhood would congregate there at Mr. Lee's counter, talking about nothing all day long, just nonstop. Once in a while they'd order something: *Lemme get a coffee*. They were people from the

neighborhood, retired electricians or older people, who used to just chill there all day long and play Lotto and wait there for conversation. The same conversation all the time too. This guy Skip, whenever he would see me, he would always start the conversation off like we had already been in the conversation. It was always about the Jets and his father and him being in the stands and Joe Namath and some kind of glory story that ended up with him explaining his pain, because we shared pain for the Jets. He would have the racing form rolled up in his pocket and his fisherman's hat on. That neighborhood really made me—it just has so many characters.

Eventually, they expanded the Key Food supermarket on the same block, and that took over Larry's and Lill's. So the Japanese restaurant on the same block, which is run by Chinese people, decided to open in the morning and double up as a short-order breakfast place because they saw how much business they could make. So now those same motherfuckers hang out at the Japanese restaurant.

✱ Stolen food is a big thing in my life. We used to throw barbecues where we would fill up a whole fucking wagon with meat at the Trade Fair or Key Food supermarket and make off with hundreds and hundreds of dollars of stolen packaged flesh. When I worked at the Key Food stocking shelves in junior high, I would steal lunch every day—they would make me a sandwich and I would throw it down my leg then go to the basement and eat it.

9. INCREDIBLE PAIRINGS

AKA

The Great Little Nuances of Life; the Partnerships; the Special **THIS** *That Always Goes with* **THAT**

A FOUNTAIN COKE—*with* THOSE LITTLE ICE PELLETS *in a* WAXED CARDBOARD CUP—*and a* SLICE *of* PIZZA.

THE ICED TEA *in the* BIG STYROFOAM CUP OR BIG PLASTIC TAKEOUT CONTAINER THAT YOU GET DELIVERED *with* NEW YORK CITY CHINESE FOOD.

THE PIECE OF FRENCH BREAD *that* CROWNS THE STREET CART SHISH KEBAB.

THE WWF WRESTLING ICE CREAM BAR *and* THE PARK.

GRILLED CHEESE *and* KETCHUP.

AREPAS *and a* JUGO DE MORA.

TEN TUBS OF ICE CREAM *with* DEPRESSION.

TAKEOUT EATEN OFF THE HOOD *of* THE CAR.

CRISPIX *and* SKIM MILK.

WENDY'S SPICY CHICKEN SANDWICH *and a* FROSTY.

ASIAN FOOD *and* AUSTRALIA.

BIG MACS *and* FAT CAMP.

BASKIN-ROBBINS *and* MINI BASEBALL HELMETS.

SUNNYDALE LEMON ICED TEA *and a* HANDBALL GAME.

HK ANDERSON PRETZELS *and* GINGER ALE, MOUNTAIN DEW, *or* ICED TEA.

FRIED CHICKEN *and* NATURAL WINE.

HOOD CHINESE FOOD *and* DUTCHES.

BURNT-CINNAMON SAUSAGE *and* NATURAL CIDER.

TING *and* a BEEF PATTY.

HOT DOUG'S *and a* CHICAGO ROOFTOP.

WHITE TRUFFLES *and* VANILLA SOFT-SERVE.

CHOCOLATE *and* LEMON ITALIAN ICE *in the* SAME CUP.

MILTON A. ABEL JR.'S CHOCOLATE CHIP COOKIES *with* SALTED HONEY BUTTER.

IMPORTANT NOTES

I.

THE WWF WRESTLING ICE CREAM BAR *and* THE PARK.

The WWF Superstars of Wrestling Ice Cream Bar was my second favorite ice cream bar in the world after the Chipwich, both of which are now extinct (though the Chipwich has made a comeback here in New York City). When the ice cream truck came by the park, those were the only things I wanted. This bar had a picture of one of the wrestlers on the cover and came with a trading card and a sticker with a quote, both of which I collected. They had a soft, shortbready-almond cookie top and a chocolate back, and they were banging. They had to change the name to WWE, because of issues with the name and the World Wildlife Fund, but whatever. (I love ice cream trucks in general. In fact, one time way back when I was playing in a baseball game, the ice cream man starts playing the song as I'm about to go up to bat. I of course go to get an ice cream, and they're looking all over for me. I run back, get up there, and hit a home run.) Another honorable mention is those icees with the faces, like Batman, or a Powerpuff Girl, where the eyeballs are gumballs. The gumballs are never chewy, because they're frozen for mad long and they just turn into this gummy dust—they're incredible.

II.

AREPAS *and a* JUGO DE MORA.

This is a combination I feel everyone should encounter in their life. An arepa is a Colombian corn cake—it's just corn, no extra sugar like one of those you get at the fair, which are also amazing. You blister it on the stovetop to where you have these pockets of charred corn action, you top it with this shredded, salty mozzarella–type Colombian cheese, and then you get a *jugo de mora*— frozen blackberries and ice blended into a slushie. You drink that together, the blistered bits from the arepa with the salty cheese against the sweet-tartness of the berry drink? It's orgasmic. For the drink, they'll ask you if you want it with ice or milk—*agua o leche*? You want it with ice. But before you get those, you have to start with *almojábana*, a little round puffball made with *cuajada* cheese and corn flour. Un-fucking-real, and you have to get it first thing when it comes out of the oven.

III.

TAKEOUT EATEN OFF THE HOOD *of* THE CAR.

Fried chicken on the hood of the car, sandwiches on the hood, pizza on the hood, pretty much anything on the hood of the car. Generally, I want to eat standing in front of the restaurant, leaning around the car parked just outside. I don't want to have to put on a blazer or eat sitting on a stool. That's what me and Meyhem and Body have been doing our whole life—never would you eat sitting down.

IV.
CRISPIX *and* SKIM MILK.

See page 18.

V.
WENDY'S SPICY CHICKEN SANDWICH *and a* FROSTY.

The Malaysians, they also know that spicy fried chicken just works with something chocolaty and cold. In Sydney, one of my favorite restaurants is Mamak—Mamak are Malaysian-Muslims originally from South India—where I always get the Malay-style spiced fried chicken (see page 198) with an icy drink made from milk and Milo chocolate malt powder.

VI.
ASIAN FOOD *and* AUSTRALIA.

Australia, man, that is where I've had some of the best Asian food of my life. It is like the most diverse place in the world to eat Asian food. There's Mamak, above, which has unbelievable food and even has one person standing there all day long making Malaysian roti, a doughy, flaky, just unbelievable thing that's

THE PIECE OF FRENCH BREAD *that* **CROWNS THE STREET CART SHISH KEBAB.**

almost like a crepe. Chef Dan Hong, who runs a Chinese-Asian-Vietnamese place called Ms. G's, also took me to this Vietnamese city called Cabramatta, about an hour west of Sydney, where his mother used to have a restaurant. People are just growing stuff in their backyards like squash flowers and banana leaves and selling it on the street. I didn't know much about good Vietnamese food, and that trip introduced me to so much ill shit—shrimp paste on sugarcane and rice paper wraps and *bún bò huê*, this spicy beef and pork noodle soup. And this place in Perth called Long Chim is also banging, and where I had some of the most incredible northern Thai food with just a little bit of Pacific Island in there. Their *larb*, or that thrown-together ground

meat salad also called *larp*—oh my god. Theirs felt like there was no meat in it, and I mean that in a good way. It was filled with lime leaves and chiles and fried crispy things and salty and sweet—you just shovel it into your mouth, you can't get enough of it, like those peanuts on the fucking bar with the lime and the chile. In reality, one of the best meals I've had in L.A. ever—at this place E.P. & L.P.—was actually really more like an Australian-Asian deal because the Chinese-Indian-Fijian chef Louis Tikaram came to L.A. from Australia, where he grew up. One of my favorite things there was smoked lamb neck with herbs like mint and basil, wrapped in lettuce leaves and dipped into some shit—oh, fuck, it was crazy, and it all tasted like being back in Perth.

VII.
BIG MACS *and* FAT CAMP.

I used to run Big Macs and candy bars at fat camp, and that's a true story—and don't fucking tell anybody, because we're going to have some issues. It was Camp Shane in New York, and it was literally like the movie *Heavyweights*. One of the counselors used to get me the stuff. Anything I wanted she would bring me, in the middle of the night sometimes, and then I would sell it off: Snickers, a bucket of fried chicken, and especially Big Macs. There were definitely kids there who lost no weight because they were just eating burgers. I stuck to it, and I actually lost about thirty or forty pounds. That counselor really broke all kinds of rules—she broke the ethics of life. She was nineteen, and I was just fourteen, but I told her I was seventeen. I lost my virginity to her the last day of camp, in a room full of boys asleep in bunk beds. It was awesome.

VIII.
BASKIN-ROBBINS *and* MINI BASEBALL HELMETS.

When I was younger, Baskin-Robbins started selling two-scoop sundaes in mini Major League Baseball helmets. You had to collect them all—it was like getting a Happy Meal, meaning sometimes you don't even really care about the ice cream, you just want another

helmet. FYI: When I was younger I liked vanilla chip, but as I got older, I became a mint chocolate chip fiend, and there is no new flavor that can stop me.

IX.
SUNNYDALE LEMON ICED TEA *and a* HANDBALL GAME.

Sunnydale Farms was a milk company from Brooklyn that sold milk, juice, and tea in milk cartons with this cool design to all the New York City delis until 2005. They had lemon tea and fruit punch—that shit was like crack. They were a handball special; after handball you'd go in the corner store and they were like twenty-five cents—or free, if you just take one and walk on out.

X.
FRIED CHICKEN *and* NATURAL WINE.

The last time I was in Australia, we ate fried chicken every night and we drank natural wine (see page 138) every night. That's all I wanted: I was addicted to that combination. We got them both from this place Belles Hot Chicken, which focuses on natural wine and fried chicken in the Nashville style, where you roll it in the dry spices after it's fried. A few days later, we did it in fucking Melbourne too, because there's a Belles Hot Chicken there too. We even had Kimchi Pete Jo, a Korean chef and

sommelier who is also Belles' natural wine consigliere, taste us through some of Australia's best natural wines on a rooftop. I was drunk off my ass—but a happy drunk, just enjoying myself—and I don't think that fried chicken has ever tasted so good, because that fucking natural wine acts like a fluffer.

XI.
HOOD ——————▶ CHINESE FOOD *and* DUTCHES.

As in asking the Chinese deliveryman to also bring up two vanilla Dutch Masters along with my General Torso's chicken. Hood Chinese is not actually hood, it's just New York City Chinese-American takeout Chinese. Do they deliver to a three-mile radius? Then it's hood Chinese.

OK, this is a big thing for me, I am not going to lie. I've switched between the brown sauce and the "light" white sauce (cornstarch, water, salt, and chicken stock) for years. I went through stages: General Tso's chicken, sesame chicken, or chicken and broccoli. I get on these kicks and I overdo it. There were points when I got sesame chicken every day for a month, then General Tso's every day for a month, then there'd be another switch-up. By then they'd know my order, and when I changed it, they would always be surprised: *Oh, different today?* It was like a *Seinfeld* episode. When you get General Torso's chicken—that's what I always call General Tso's—all you get are three lousy little pieces of broccoli, and they always taste

like fish because they steam them in the shrimp dumpling basket. With the brown and the white chickens, the broccoli is sautéed together with everything else.

XII.
BURNT-CINNAMON SAUSAGE *and* NATURAL CIDER.

State Bird Provisions in San Francisco makes two of the best things I have ever had in my life: potato chips with salmon roe cured with Meyer lemon and served with crème fraîche, and this Thai-style Chiang Mai sausage with burnt cinnamon and sour fermented rice. They served it to me with a spontaneous, funky, natural hard apple cider, the alcoholic version,

one where the yeasts that fermented the apples were wild and left to do their thing. That might be the most incredible pairing that I've ever had in my life, honestly, or at least at that moment it made me feel like it was.

← XIII.
TING *and a* BEEF PATTY.

In New York, a lot of people who know nothing about Jamaican food know about Jamaican beef patties from New York City bodegas or the pizzeria. You'd get the beef patty split open and heat it up with cheese or with pepperoni. It's no longer Jamaican, really—it becomes like a true New York beef patty right there, because everybody used to get a beef patty with cheese—everybody. If I am being straight up, that was my first encounter with Jamaican food. My feeling is the best Jamaican patty

spot anywhere is the Jamaican Flavors window on 165th Street in Queens outside the Colosseum Mall, a very popular thing in rap lore. Every rapper used to go there to get their sneakers and their clothing and jewelry. Downstairs there's almost like a little mini Diamond District. At Jamaican Flavors you can see that the patties are handmade. You can see the fat between the flake. You get them with curry chicken, jerk chicken, callaloo and salt fish, spicy beef, regular beef, BBQ, and so on, and they have a cooler of tropical Mistic fruit drinks and Ting on the sidewalk. You always gotta get some sort of punch with the patties, and I get the Ting, the Jamaican beverage of choice, always found in a small green glass bottle. It's a sparkling grapefruit soda—I usually don't like grapefruit, but I love Ting. Jamaicans are apparently the only ones left who drink Mistic, those ridiculously sweet rainbow-colored fruit drinks. Drink too many of them and you'll end up having to cut your foot off and walk around like Lieutenant Dan from *Forrest Gump*.

XIV.
HOT DOUG'S *and a* CHICAGO ROOFTOP.

I feel like something died in Chicago when Hot Doug's closed down in 2014. It's a shame. Hot Doug's was like a cuisine unto itself: To call what Doug Sohn did hot dogs or even sausages just does not do them justice. Each of his works was like a snowflake, found only once in nature, like the foie gras–and–Sauternes duck sausage with truffle aioli, foie gras mousse, and sea salt, with a side of the duck fat fries that have that next-level crunch. We got into town three weeks before he was closing—I had nightmares I would miss my chance—and the line took four hours. We ordered fifteen different hot dogs and ate them on the rooftop balcony of the Michael Jordan suite at the Public Hotel Chicago overlooking Lake Shore Drive.

XV. →
WHITE TRUFFLES *and* VANILLA SOFT-SERVE.

I've been putting olive oil on ice cream since forever, but at Lilia in Brooklyn, Chef Missy Robbins showed me how she puts truffles on top of soft-serve with olive oil, honey, and sea salt. Most vanilla ice cream is too rich and too delicious, but Häagen-Dazs is a good canvas for pretty much anything. Truffles are best on plain vanilla soft-serve, like at McDonald's or the one at Lilia. Usually with white truffles you just shave them onto something, but I feel like you have to activate them as well, with that little bit of olive oil and sea salt. Like at Babbo in Manhattan, where they do the pasta with white truffles with hot butter, a little bit of cheese, and salt.

(It's crazy, but the smell of that white truffle pasta reminds me of those little twenty-five-cent bags of Wise potato chips my mother used to get at Costco—that first initial blast of smell that's just been bubbling in the bag so that when you pop it open— *whoa.* My mother and I would go explore the Costco on Old Country Road in Long Island, so long ago it was still called Price Club. At Costco I got a see-through jade green beeper

with a gray clip, Kirkland Signature cashmere sweaters, the Sega Genesis pack with *Sonic the Hedgehog* and *Altered Beast* and one controller, and a mountain bike. Mainly I would wander off and taste all the samples—you couldn't let me in the cake area or the croissant aisle—and pull the disappearing kid shit. Then when I couldn't find my mother, I would follow the sound of the jingle of keys on this silver key chain she had.)

XVI.
CHOCOLATE *and* LEMON ITALIAN ICE *in the* SAME CUP.

The chocolate-lemon mix is my thing—in Italian ices or even gelato. It used to be chocolate and cherry, but the lemon is better. The chocolate is rich and nutty, then you get that bright lemon that cuts right through it. When eating ices, you must also chew on the paper to get the last bit. Shooting a Super Soaker while eating an ice during the summer is also a must.

XVII.
MILTON A. ABEL JR.'S CHOCOLATE CHIP COOKIES *with* SALTED HONEY BUTTER.

Milton is an amazing person and pastry chef. He's worked at the best of the best—like French Laundry and

Per Se—and his dad was a famous jazz musician in St. Louis, *the* Milton A. Abel Sr. I first had his chocolate chip cookies and honey butter with salt when he was working at Amass in Copenhagen. They did this American-style barbecue for us outside, and Milton made the perfect chocolate chip cookie—soft inside, with a crispy edge and so many chips it's like a chocolate-stuffed cookie—but also corn bread with honey butter, which he made with really good butter, Danish honey, and a touch of salt. I put the honey butter on the cookie. A year or so later, I was in Copenhagen, it was late, he DMed me, and he straight-up made me some cookies and honey butter at midnight and brought them over to the hotel. These are Milton's secret recipes (see page 51). They don't cut corners, but that's why they're so sick.

MILTON SAYS: "I was a young *demi chef de partie* at the French Laundry and I made corn bread for the staff meal. I am very proud of my corn bread. I was excited for Chef Keller to taste it for the first time. I spied him going through the chow line and my excitement grew. He came around the corner with a piece of corn bread in his hand toward my station and said in a jovial way, *Where the honey butter, Chef?* Always gotta have honey butter with corn bread. From that day forward I have never served corn bread without honey butter . . . ever . . . no matter where I have worked. When Action Bronson came to Amass for the BBQ, I made chocolate chip cookies, corn bread, and honey butter. He took the combo to the next level by putting the cookies and honey butter together."

Milton A. Abel Jr.'s Chocolate Chip Cookies and Salted Honey Butter

The perfect cookie.

MAKES ABOUT 24 COOKIES

MILTON SAYS: "A great chef who I worked with at the French Laundry passed down this chocolate chip recipe to me when we were chefs de partie together. I normally don't place great importance on keeping recipes secret, as knowledge is meant to be shared, but for some reason I have with this one. . . . It's time to share this recipe."

2½ cups (371 g) packed all-purpose flour
1 teaspoon baking soda
1 teaspoon salt
1 cup (2 sticks / 227 g) unsalted butter, softened
1¾ cups (364 g) packed dark brown sugar
2 large eggs
1 tablespoon vanilla bean paste
1 pound (455 g) chocolate chips
Salted Honey Butter, for spreading on the cookie

1. In a large bowl, whisk together the flour, baking soda, and salt.

2. In a stand mixer fitted with a paddle attachment, cream the butter and sugar at medium speed until fluffy and well blended.

3. Add the eggs and vanilla paste and mix until fully incorporated.

4. Reduce the mixer speed to low, add the dry ingredients, and mix until the dough just comes together.

5. Add the chocolate chips and mix until they are just worked into the dough. (Milton says: "The quality and flavor of chocolate chips also make a difference. I like to use a mix of milk and dark chocolate. I don't expect you to put Valrhona in your cookies—I do, lol—but use something you really enjoy eating. Hell, it is Chef BamBamBaklava's cookbook we are talking about here!")

6. Line a baking sheet with parchment paper. Divide the dough into 2-ounce (60 g) portions and roll them into rounds with your hands. Put them in one layer on the prepared baking sheet (touching slightly is fine) and chill for 30 minutes. After they are chilled, store them in the freezer in a zip-top bag if you're not baking them in the next day or two. Meanwhile, position a rack in the middle of the oven and preheat the oven to 350°F (175°C), or set the oven to 325°F (160°C) on a convection setting.

7. Line a second sheet with parchment paper, place 6 dough rounds on it, and flatten them slightly, keeping about 2 inches (5 cm) of space around them on all sides. This distance is important for timing and texture—don't be tempted to squeeze more in.

8. Place the cookies in the oven and bake for 8 minutes, then rotate the sheet and bake for an additional 4 minutes, or until the cookies are golden brown around the edges and look like they are just set on the top. (In a conventional oven, bake one sheet of cookies at a time for best results. If you're using a convection oven, you can bake two sheets at once.)

9. For softer cookies, remove the cookies from the oven and allow them to finish cooking on the hot baking sheet while you set up the next batch on a fresh sheet. They will be loose at first, but give them time, they'll set up. If you like a slightly crispier edge to your cookies, bake them for 1 additional minute after rotation, but still let them carry-over cook on the sheet. (Milton says: "The carry-over cooking is really the key to me. It creates that crispy edge and soft center effect that makes the difference. If you bake them all the way in the oven, after carry-over cooking they get too crispy, in my opinion.")

Salted Honey Butter

MAKES ABOUT 2 CUPS (379 G)

1 cup (2 sticks / 227 g) unsalted butter, at room temperature
½ cup (150 g) honey
½ teaspoon salt

Place all the ingredients in a large bowl and beat with a stiff rubber spatula until light and slightly whipped. To get it really light and fluffy, you could also use a stand mixer fitted with a paddle attachment. ●

10. TACO BELL'S CHEESY GORDITA CRUNCH

They must put some sort of drug in the Cheesy Gordita Crunch at Taco Bell, something that makes you crave it. Plus it's the perfect blend of everything I like: I love crunch, I love softness, and I love when it's put together in between cheese. There's the outside wrap—it's fluffy and soft—then there's the cheese, and then there's the hard shell. It adheres together and becomes one thing, like a catcher's mitt of taco meat. They put a beautiful little sauce on it, some kind of ranch thing, and you have to get extra cheese. This is usually eaten at two in the morning while driving around the Bayside area of Queens, near Northern Boulevard and Utopia Parkway where the Taco Bell is. You put the Fire hot sauce on it—once across the whole thing, then on each bite—and you just go in without shame, ravenous and rabid like you haven't eaten in two weeks.

11. CRISPY RICE

I am addicted to crunchy rice. When you make rice in a lot of cultures, people fight over the bottom of the pot, that burnt bit. It's *pegao* to Puerto Ricans—*pegao* means stuck together—and *concon* to Dominicans, or in Korea it's *nurungji*. I love that shit. I think all the Rice Krispies I had early on did me in. In Japan we went to Tokyo's Koreatown after one of my shows, and I had *bibimbap* where they flipped it and put all the crunchy rice that forms on the bottom of the hot stone bowl on the top as they served it. I was just eating humongous squares of crispy rice with my chopsticks—the biggest piece of nurungji I'd had in my life. If there was a way to make the entire rice like that, it would be life-changing. My nonna used to make something that was close: She would roast a chicken in raw short-grain rice, like the kind you use for paella, and the rice would soak up the chicken juices and fat while the chicken was roasting. After the chicken was done, she would take it out and let the rice cook by itself in the oven. It would get dry and crunchy on the top. I've tried to mimic it many times, but I've never been able to perfect it. It's very special, those little bombs of crispy chicken rice.

CRUNCHY RICE SLANG

PEGAO
PUERTO RICO

CONCÓN
DOMINICAN REPUBLIC

GUOBA
CHINA

NURUNGJI
KOREA

TAHDIG
IRAN

HIKAKEH
IRAQ

RIZ BRÛLÉ
FRANCE

RASPADO
SOUTHWESTERN COLOMBIA

12. LEGUMES

I am heavy on legumes in general. In my house, chickpeas were always served dry and roasted Albanian-style and you would eat them as a snack—we called them *leblebija*, which sounds like *leb-leb-leah*. There was always a bowl of them in the crib. You could have salted ones and unsalted ones—I loved the unsalted ones. You know how your mouth feels when you eat a lot of saltine crackers? The unsalted ones used to do that, and I really like that. I make a lot of legumes a lot of ways these days trying to be healthy, but really my love for them started from being Albanian. I stew them, I smash them, I make hummus. I put them into little samosa-like cakes, and I do Jamaican-style curried chickpeas with coconut milk and sweet plantains. I also make crispy chickpeas, the illest bar snack ever—you treat them like *cacahuates*, those Mexican-style fried peanuts with salt, chili powder, the spice mix, and a squeeze of lime. But I never really had chickpeas soft, not even boiled or in hummus, until I was older. Instead we always made *pasul*, which is just big white beans with parsley, paprika, and Vegeta, the Balkan spice blend and vegetable soup mix that's like dried vegetables and MSG. My nonna would make it perfectly—she would even pick out all the bean skin imperfections with her hands.

PASUL

Very simple, but very good.

SERVES 2

My nonna's way to flavor beans was to cook some paprika, onion, and parsley in olive oil, and then stir that right into the beans with some Vegeta before it goes into the oven. We would serve pasul with smoked meats or sprinkled with feta, and we would all eat it at the table in the living room straight out of the *tepsia*, or the circular metal dish Albanians cook everything in. No spoon—we use the bread as our spoon.

½ pound (250 g) cannellini beans
Salt
Vegeta
¼ cup (60 ml) extra virgin olive oil, plus extra for garnishing
⅓ cup (35 g) sliced white onion
½ cup (25 g) parsley leaves
2 teaspoons good-quality paprika

1. Soak beans in 6 cups (1.4 L) water and 1 tablespoon salt for 8 hours or overnight.

2. Drain and rinse the beans, then put them in a medium saucepan with a pinch of salt and an inch or so (2.5 cm) of water to cover. Simmer over medium-low heat until cooked through, about 45 minutes to an hour.

3. Preheat the oven to 450°F (230°C).

4. Using a slotted spoon, add the beans to a small baking dish that fits them snugly, like a terra-cotta round or a small cast-iron pan. Add a few spoonfuls of their cooking water—so it is about ¼ inch (6 mm) up the side of the beans—and sprinkle them with a teaspoon of Vegeta. Stir the Vegeta into the liquid and then taste it, adding more Vegeta (and salt, if you happen to have accidentally bought the MSG-free Vegeta) until it tastes amazing. Set the beans aside.

5. Heat the olive oil in a small skillet over medium heat. Add the onion and cook until it just begins to soften and smell aromatic—maybe a minute—then add the parsley and do the same. Stir in the paprika—the oil should look red. Pour this over the beans, then gently stir it in.

6. Bake the beans until the bean water is bubbling intensely and has mainly evaporated and the top of the beans begin to look dry and shaggy, about 30 minutes.

7. Drizzle with more olive oil and eat with bread—topped with feta it's even better.

This is supposed to be the spoon.

Fuck this spoon. At home we would only use the bread as the spoon.

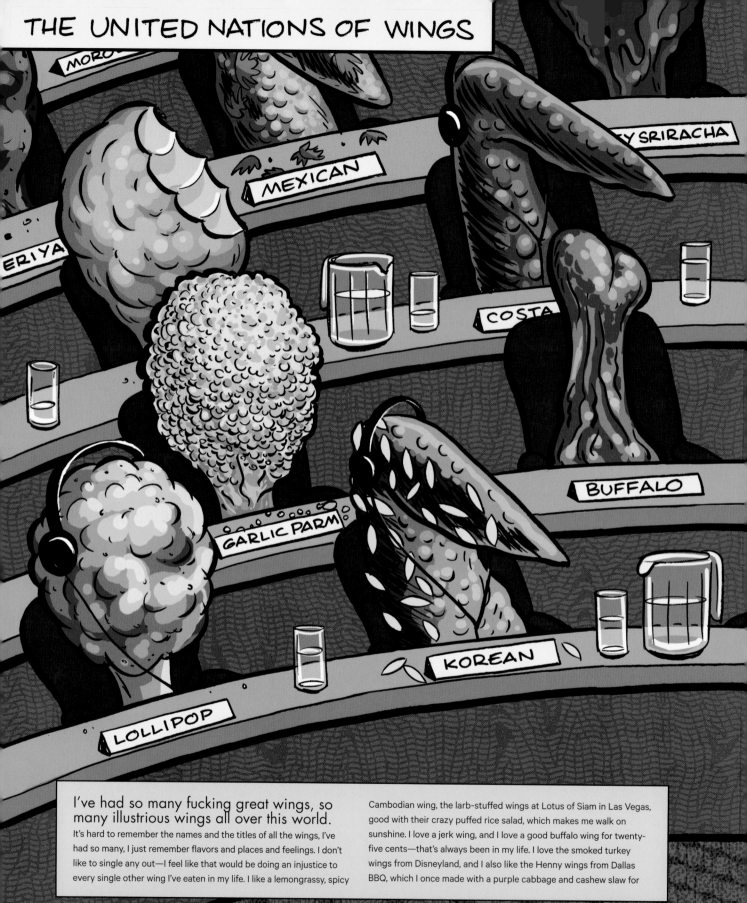

MOROC...

MEXICAN

...Y SRIRACHA

...ERIYA

COSTA...

BUFFALO

GARLIC PARM

KOREAN

LOLLIPOP

I've had so many fucking great wings, so many illustrious wings all over this world.

It's hard to remember the names and the titles of all the wings, I've had so many, I just remember flavors and places and feelings. I don't like to single any out—I feel like that would be doing an injustice to every single other wing I've eaten in my life. I like a lemongrassy, spicy

Cambodian wing, the larb-stuffed wings at Lotus of Siam in Las Vegas, good with their crazy puffed rice salad, which makes me walk on sunshine. I love a jerk wing, and I love a good buffalo wing for twenty-five cents—that's always been in my life. I love the smoked turkey wings from Disneyland, and I also like the Henny wings from Dallas BBQ, which I once made with a purple cabbage and cashew slaw for

13. Wings

Fuck, That's Delicious. I got that from my homeboy Tom Gould from Melbourne, who is also the director of photography for the TV show. Early on he and his homeboys, they had this tradition that when I visited Melbourne they would always make little chicken niblets and slaw. When you don't really know anybody in a foreign place and these dudes take you into their crib and make chicken and slaw, it's great. Some of the best wings I have ever had were from Detroit—I played at this venue called Saint Andrew's Hall, and right across the street is a bar called Sweetwater Tavern, where they have these legendary smoked and fried wings. We got them catered—it was a tray of at least a couple hundred of them, and when we were done there were only twenty left. It was, in fact, legendary shit.

OLD-SCHOOL ICE CREAM SHOPS

14.
CONDITORI LA GLACE →

B. 1870, COPENHAGEN

I'll never forget their *sportskage*, or sports cake. It was speckled with chipped pieces of caramel, and the body was light, fluffy gorgeousness—no wonder they've been open for so many years. They have a 125-year-old ice cream churner, which is old and humongous and gorgeous.

15.
MARGIE'S CANDIES

B. 1921, CHICAGO

Margie's is a staple in Chicago, a must-visit: It's stuck in time. I love this place and their big-ass banana splits.

This is the extreme version.

16.
EDDIE'S SWEET SHOP →

B. 1909, FOREST HILLS, QUEENS

I started going to Eddie's when I went to junior high school nearby. I go now just to feel like a kid again, even though they've renovated lightly, unlike La Glace or Margie's. I get malted milk shakes, banana splits, all the candies that you want in the world. You can do a cannonball into their bowl of whipped cream: It's very, very tall. ●

17. GOGO'S COFFEE CAKE

You must use none other than Bonne Maman raspberry preserves.

SERVES 12 TO 14

This, along with a peach pie and a chocolate raspberry layer cake, is one of the three desserts I have seen the most in my life because my mom makes them all the time. She is an excellent baker—for a while she even made cakes for weddings and parties, like a red velvet cake for two hundred people that she had to lay out on her bed, it was so many layers. I usually helped her do the sugar work. My mother sometimes makes this with crumble top instead of crunchy drizzles of ganache, but I don't like that version, and we always, always used Bonne Maman preserves, I have never seen her use another brand. I also don't think I have ever actually had a real piece of coffee cake; I just pick at the crispy edges all around the top instead, where it's like a cookie.

Nonstick cooking spray
1 cup (2 sticks / 225 g) unsalted butter, at room temperature
1¼ cups (250 g) granulated sugar
2 teaspoons baking powder
½ teaspoon baking soda
3 large eggs
1½ teaspoons vanilla extract
2¼ cups (280 g) all-purpose flour
1 cup (240 ml) sour cream
¼ cup (60 g) cane sugar
2 tablespoons ground cinnamon
6 tablespoons (100 g) mini chocolate chips

½ cup (120 ml) Bonne Maman raspberry preserves
¼ to ⅓ cup (60 to 75 ml) Gloria's Chocolate Ganache Glaze (opposite), warmed
1 tablespoon powdered sugar

1. Preheat the oven to 350°F (175°C) and coat a 10- or 12-cup Bundt pan with cooking spray. My mother almost always uses the plain disposable aluminum foil kind, because she so often gives them away.

2. In a stand mixer fitted with a paddle attachment, mix the butter and granulated sugar on medium-high speed until they are light and creamy, about 2 minutes.

3. With the machine on a slightly lower speed, add the baking powder, baking soda, one egg at a time, and the vanilla and beat until blended, about 1 minute. Add ⅓ of the flour, followed by ⅓ of the sour cream, then repeat two times, making sure each addition is blended in before adding the next. Turn the mixer off and, using a rubber spatula, scrape the bowl and the paddle. Mix on medium speed for another 30 seconds, or until the mixture is smooth.

4. In a small bowl, stir together the cane sugar and cinnamon.

5. Add ⅓ of the batter to the Bundt pan, distributing it in dollops around the inside of the pan. Spread and smooth the batter even with a spatula and sprinkle 2 tablespoons of the cinnamon-sugar mixture and 2 tablespoons of chocolate chips over the top. Repeat two more times, topping each addition of batter with 2 tablespoons of the cinnamon-sugar and 2 tablespoons of chocolate chips.

6. Place in the oven and bake for 20 minutes, then add the preserves, dolloping it on by the spoonful around the inner ring of the top of the batter so that you make a circle halfway between the outer edge and the center hole of the pan.

7. Bake for another 40 minutes, or until a tester inserted into the middle comes out clean. Let cool completely on a wire rack before glazing. If you're using a plain disposable pan like my mother, you cool it in the pan, then glaze the top of the cake. If you're using a fancy pan with a design, invert the cake from the pan, to cool, and glaze the bottom.

8. Use a spoon to drizzle the chocolate ganache glaze in thin ribbons back and forth across the top of the cake, then sprinkle on the powdered sugar. Slice and serve.

GLORIA'S CHOCOLATE GANACHE GLAZE

Anything glazed* is ill. That's a quote right there.

MAKES 4 CUPS (1 L)

*

Hams, doughnuts, brioche, crème brûlée, Pop-Tarts, etc. Is any food with glaze ever bad?

2 cups (480 ml) heavy cream
½ cup (100 g) sugar
3 cups (489 g) semisweet chocolate chips
2 tablespoons unsalted butter, at room temperature

1. Heat the cream in a double boiler over medium-high heat (you can also use a heatproof bowl set over a pot filled with a few inches of simmering water).

2. When the cream forms a skin on the top and tiny bubbles begin to break the surface, mix in the sugar, stirring constantly with a heatproof spatula until it dissolves.

3. When the mixture begins to steam and show tiny bubbles beneath the surface, add the chocolate chips and stir constantly until the chips have melted and the mixture is smooth, at least 10 minutes, likely more. (Says my mom: "If you don't pay attention, it's ruined.")

4. Remove the pan from the heat, add the butter, and stir until it is totally incorporated.

5. Let cool slightly before using. The glaze can be kept, refrigerated, for up to 2 weeks; bring to room temperature or gently reheat over a double boiler before using.

18. FOOD MAGAZINES BY THE TOILET

It's kind of disgusting, but gorgeous at the same time.
I used to buy my magazines and put them there too, like *Muscular Development* when I was on so much steroids I was a beast. This is how I was introduced to *Gourmet* magazine, *Edible Queens*—I would read for hours when I wasn't shitting. I found myself sitting down to take a piss just so I could read *Gourmet* magazine. And if you didn't have magazines by the toilet, then I really can't fuck with you: Reading material by the toilet is very, very important.

FOOD MAGAZINES

TOILET

19.

Grønsagen

Grønsagen is a legendary restaurant that pretty much feeds the entire community of Freetown Christiania, which is this giant forty-year-old squat in an old military barracks in the middle of Copenhagen. There's a special vibe at Grønsagen, which means "the vegetable." Everything is made by volunteers—they're just the people who live there. It's like Momma's home cooking for the entire neighborhood. They have organic vegetables for sale and a different rotating menu of crazy delicious foods served homemade buffet style by the pound, where you just go up and get your food on mismatched plates and then you eat it at mismatched tables and you're happy. Meat lasagna, which is really fucking incredible, vegan cakes and hummus, and the fried zucchini patties are all favorites of mine. You know you're going to get a good, wholesome meal there, something healthy and cheap. And you're definitely going to have a good time, because in Christiania you can buy weed and you can smoke it anywhere you want.

That's Jan, one of the friendly guiding lights of Christiania.

MORE COPENHAGEN: To the left, WarPigs Brewpub for Texas-style barbecue with Hot Dog John. Above is a burger under the bridge, and the cellar of WarPigs where we tasted very long–aged beer in different types of barrels. (This one is a Hennessy.) At right, a whole fish, also eaten under the Knippelsbro bridge at a natural wine dinner. Then the bourbon milkshake at WarPigs, and a Turkish sandwich made with a bunch of fucking beef at the Copenhagen Street Food market.

69

20.

A HAMBURGER MADE ANY TYPE OF WAY THAT IS POSSIBLE

For the longest time, I thought a burger had onions and parsley in it. But eventually I came to realize that I was lied to as a child, and what they were really making me was an Albanian dish called *cevapi**—though we pronounce it more like *chepapi*. I didn't know that a hamburger was a hamburger until I got a real one years later, because my hamburgers always came with mad shit in it. The funny thing is, anytime I get a burger like that elsewhere—with stuff in the patty—I always hate it. I don't like a flavored patty. I don't like when you put adobo in it, or herbs or any other seasoning. I don't even put black pepper on the patty, even though I love black pepper. It just bothers me—you can't call it a burger when you do that. You have to call it something else, like cevapi, or a *chimi* (see page 88). I love a pure hamburger, but other than that you can make it with any thing, any way: steamed, fried, grilled, griddled, broiled. That's actually what my mom used to make me for lunch: broiled burgers on square soft white bread.

HAMBURGERS WITH BLACK TRUFFLES AND 24-MONTH COMTÉ

Truffles are only fancy to us because we don't live where they come from.

SERVES 4

These days the purest patty I can get is from Marlow & Daughters butcher shop in Brooklyn—the meat is just phenomenal, and it's also aged gorgeously. Aged meat browns up amazingly, and if you let it sit out and dry just a little further—an hour or two on the counter—it really crisps and crunches on the outside when you cook it, like brown little crystals. I may add some fancy things to my burger, but it's simple fancy because it's just two things—truffle and imported Comté cheese—that are going to take this burger to the next level.

1 pound (450 g) dry-aged ground beef
Extra virgin olive oil
Flaky sea salt
1 small black truffle
8 ounces (225 g) 24-month-old
    Comté, preferably Marcel Petite
    Fort St. Antoine

4 Martin's Famous Potato Rolls
¼ cup (½ stick) softened butter

1. Form the meat into 4 loose patties and set them on a plate or a sheet pan. The key is making them light—don't pack them down.

2. Heat a cast-iron skillet over medium-high heat. When you're ready to cook the burgers, drizzle a little oil in the bottom of the pan and salt one side of the burgers heavily with the sea salt so you'll get that crunch on the outside.

3. Place the burgers, salt side down, in the pan and then salt the other side. They will begin to smoke, so be prepared. When the burgers are crunchy and brown on one side— maybe 5 to 7 minutes, if your pan is really hot—flip them over and cook until the other side is brown.

4. While the patties cook, shave the truffle and the cheese into thin slices. When the patties are almost done, cover each patty with a thin layer of shaved truffles and a layer of shaved cheese. Let the cheese melt slightly and then remove the burgers to a cutting board or plate to rest.

5. Turn the heat on the pan to low and butter the top of each bun and both of the insides. Close the buns, gently place them bottom side down into the hot pan, and let them cook just until the bottom is nicely browned. Flip them over and brown the top.

6. When the buns are ready, add the burgers, top them with any leftover truffle and cheese, and eat.

✱ **CEVAPI** is ground meat with onions and parsley, and it is juicy and a little spongy because there's baking soda in it, and it's fucking unbelievably delicious. It's Albanian street food: You usually get ten pieces, and it comes with a side of chopped onions, it comes with bread, and it comes with *ajvar*, which is roasted eggplant, tomatoes, peppers, and shit like that pureed into a dip type of deal. I was taught you put a little salt on the side, and a little bit of crushed red pepper flakes, and then you just dip each cevapi slightly into each spice, kind of like the Moroccan lamb kebabs on page 137. That's the way I like to eat it. In Macedonia, where my family lives, you make a hundred of these things in the summertime at a barbecue and they go like wildfire.

For the best crust let your meat rest out at room temperature, and then salt it right before you cook it.

21

TOOTH-PICKS

My favorite part of eating is picking my teeth. My family is a family of teeth pickers: My grandparents on both sides, my father, and my mother. Man, do we pick our teeth. There's nothing better after eating something like jerk chicken, getting into the crevasses in the back of your mouth—it's so satisfying. (Sometimes I even like to hurt my gums with the toothpick, and I know I'm not the only one.) A business card can be used, or a MetroCard, or the plastic cellophane wrapping on the cigarette package, the little pants. I saw my Albanian grandparents use that many times. That's hard-core teeth picking right there.

DIFFERENT TYPES OF TOOTHPICKS

The plastic ones with the floss already on them. These are my favorite toothpicks in the history of life. My mother always picks her teeth with these.

The ones in little packs with the medicated tea tree oil, which invigorates the gums.

The round wood ones.

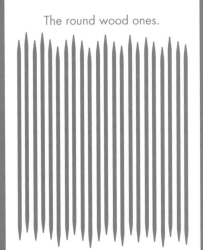

The square wood ones that I don't really like that you get in Europe, usually.

One-sided picks, where there's one with only one side with a point. These I don't like, because then I end up having to break them in half to try to make a second point.

The party ones that look like plastic swords or have frilly ends.

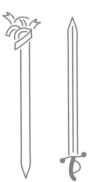

The plastic ones with spikes on one end that go in between your teeth—it looks like mascara or a grill brush. (Hey, you gotta get all that shit off your grill.)

A MetroCard.

Anyone's business card.

Plastic wrapping off a cigarette package.

22. EXPLOSIVE CHICKEN

The first time I had explosive chicken was at Z & Y Restaurant, a Szechuan place in San Francisco's Chinatown that wouldn't let us film inside. We got four or five plates of it to go and ate it on the pier. I woke up in the morning and ate some more—I ended up having it at least four more times as it is fucking incredible, just crispy nuggets of fried chicken with Szechuan peppercorns and fried chiles all over the place. I'm addicted to that Szechuan peppercorn—the numbness it delivers. A few weeks later, we were filming in Tokyo and stumbled onto a spicy food festival. After that, I was just craving that mouth-numbing chicken from San Francisco, so my friend found me a Szechuan restaurant in Tokyo. So I had Chinese chicken every single night I was in Japan with a thing of white rice. It was the most incredible time of my life.

EXPLOSIVE CHICKEN

This is the chicken of
all fucking chickens.

SERVES 4

I made this on *The Rachael Ray Show*. Some places call it chicken with pepper, some Chongqing Chicken. I call it Explosive Chicken, just like Z & Y.* Don't marinate this chicken longer than fifteen minutes—if you leave it too long, it's going to be overpowering and it's going to taste like that Japanese Sakura teriyaki chicken from the mall. Which I love, don't get me wrong, but for this you want a totally different taste.

✳ Last time we went to Z & Y we waited almost an hour for takeout, so I wandered off down to the corner to Quickly, which is a bubble tea spot with a bunch of fried things on the menu. I decided to order an almond milk tea, the popcorn chicken, Chinese corn dogs, and fried sweet bananas in spring rolls, and let me tell you something, it was as satisfying as any meal I've had ever, probably. The popcorn chicken was done so perfectly—there were pieces of all types of white and dark meat, then you sprinkle a hot chile powder on it. They have a bag for it, and then you close it and shake. Some young Asian dude walked in and said, *Yo, I can't believe you're at the Quickly, man. That's why you're my hero.*

FOR THE MARINADE AND CHICKEN
½ cup (120 ml) soy sauce
½ cup (120 ml) rice vinegar
¼ cup (50 g) sugar
1½ pounds (680 g) boneless, skinless chicken thighs

FOR THE SPICE MIXTURE
1 cup (60 g) Szechuan peppercorns, divided use
⅓ cup (60 g) sugar
1 tablespoon salt

FOR THE DREDGE AND FRY
1½ cups (220 g) rice flour
1½ cups (190 g) cornstarch
2 to 3 quarts (2 to 3 L) canola oil
3 cups (720 ml) cold seltzer water

FOR THE FINISHED DISH
2 green onions, white and green parts, cut into 2-inch (5-cm) pieces
1 cup (30 g) dried Szechuan chiles
½ bunch fresh cilantro, tough stems removed, roughly chopped
White rice, as a side

1. Make the marinade: Combine the soy sauce, vinegar, and sugar in a large bowl and whisk to dissolve the sugar.

2. Cut the chicken thighs into large chunks—nice chopstick-size pieces, about six per thigh—place them in the marinade, and leave for 15 minutes but no longer. A short dunk softens the chicken just enough and the flavor won't be overpowering.

3. Make the spice mixture: Use a spice grinder or mortar and pestle to grind all but 2 tablespoons of the peppercorns. Stir together the ground peppercorns, the sugar, and salt and set it aside.

4. Fill a Dutch oven about halfway up the sides with oil and heat it over medium-high heat to 325°F (165°C).

5. In a large bowl, whisk together the rice flour and cornstarch for the dredge, then whisk in the seltzer. Line a baking sheet with paper towels.

6. Drain the chicken from the marinade. Working with a few pieces at a time, dunk the chicken into the dredge, shake off the excess, and fry until lightly browned, crispy, and cooked through, about 5 to 7 minutes. As the pieces are done, remove them with a slotted spoon and set them on the prepared baking sheet, then sprinkle them on all sides with a little spice mixture. We could stop here and it would still taste good, but we're not going to stop here.

7. Add 1 tablespoon of oil to a large skillet or wok and heat over medium-high heat. When the oil and pan are very hot, add the green onions, the reserved whole peppercorns, the chiles, and a sprinkle of spice mixture. Toss for a second or two until the chiles smell fragrant, then add the chicken pieces. Cook, tossing often, until the chicken is heated through, 1 to 2 minutes.

8. Serve topped with the cilantro and a side of hot white rice.

In San Francisco, clockwise from top left: Explosive chicken. State Bird Provisions. Burma Superstar's chile-fried lamb. Piñatas: Body chose a dinosaur because it's his archnemesis—he doesn't believe in them. The Bay Bridge, piñatas smashed in Bay Bridge park, and then there I am on the balcony with Avirex leather. A burrito up top, the gyro from Souvla below.

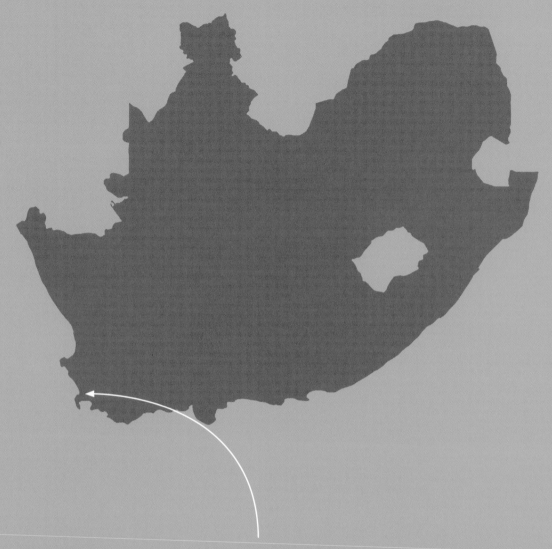

23.

MZOLI'S

In South Africa, on one of my early tours, I ate at a place from the side of the road in Cape Town called Mzoli's, an incredible open-fire South African pit barbecue place, which South Africans call *braai*. Braai is both the grilling and the grill itself. The meat's in the front when you walk in, just sitting there in piles—different types of coiled African sausages, cuts, and meats that you never see here. You pick your meat and then bring it into the back in big metal bowls or a cardboard box, where the braai master cooks it in the fire pit. They give you a plate of *pap*, which is like big grit cakes, a chopped vegetable salad, and one knife to cut all the meat. You eat with your hands, and you have beer and meat and pap and salad, and that's it. It's fucking tremendous.

24.
PIPI-KAULA AND OPIHI

Two things blew me away on my last trip to Hawaii, and both were traditional native Hawaiian things, before all the Pacific Rim fusion hit. One was **PIPIKAULA** short ribs, cooked like moist jerky. They're cut thick across the bone instead of in between the bones, so you get little nuggets of meat and bone on each piece. Those are marinated and hung to dry out over the stove, crisped up in cast iron, and served with Hawaiian chile pepper water. The second was **OPIHI**, little baby mollusks where the outside has the texture of abalone, and then in the middle it's like sea urchin roe: Unreal. They only grow on the rocks—you have to dive for them, and it's very dangerous. They're pretty much a national fucking treasure, like gold. Both of these I had for the first time at Helena's Hawaiian Food, this amazing old roadside joint in Honolulu.

Surfers call this "Gas Chambers" because it's the shallowest break in Oahu's Sandy Beach, right on to sand. All the rest are out at sea.

SANDWICHES

THE TWO TO ORDER FROM A NEW YORK DELI

25.

The bodega, the New York deli, it's all the same thing—the corner store. I really started in with deli in high school, because my best subject at school was lunch. The football team, which I was on, would hang out there, and my friend would order a made-up sandwich to get everything everyone else was getting—cream cheese and jelly, or sausage, egg, and cheese—on one sandwich. Like bacon, egg, sausage patties, ham, and cheese on a buttered bagel with cream cheese and jelly. He was just fucking around, but it turned out to be good. Today I eat two specific sandwiches from a New York deli: The first is a Philly cheesesteak from a good Akh deli, meaning a good Arabic deli (*akhi* is Arabic for "my brother," which is how you greet the guy behind the counter at an Arabic deli; at a Spanish deli, you say *papi*). Arabic delis usually make an amazing Philly cheesesteak on garlic bread. I think that's a New York thing—to differentiate their cheesesteak from a Philly cheesesteak, they put it on a garlic hero, and they usually give you the untraditional choice of mozzarella or American. I like it with mozzarella and jalapeños. The second is beef salami with American cheese, mayo, and hot sauce on a roll.

Specifically: One fried egg, with or without bacon, salt, pepper, ketchup. More ketchup on the side, for smearing. I want to elaborate on the eggs: First off, they can never be browned unless it's a fried egg—an egg white browned is fine. But when you start making scrambled eggs that are fucking browned, you're burning the protein and it makes for a disgusting flavor, and I hate it. I also hate egg sandwiches where the egg is folded up on top of itself four or five times, to the point where you feel like you're eating a fucking Big Mac and you can't even get your mouth around it. That's not poppin'. There must only be one layer of that, one layer of this, that's it. You can find the perfect egg and cheese on a roll at most local New York City bodegas, but you will have to explain how you want it.

26.

EGG AND CHEESE ON A ROLL

27. THE CHIMI

I've been eating Dominican food my whole life—going uptown to Washington Heights with Body to buy weed. It's a ritual, actually: Every time we went we would have to have the twenty-four-hour Dominican buffet on Dyckman Street, and we would have to have the sandwich from La China. La China is a Dominican *frituras* and *chimichurri* truck that parks late-night at 178th Street and Amsterdam Avenue near Highbridge Park in Manhattan, always with so many cars double-parked outside. Frituras is just shit that is fried: pig ears, pork skin, potato croquettes, little Dominican empanadas called *pastelitos,* the *tostones.* Puerto Ricans do the same thing; they call it *cuchifritos.* Their chimichurri sandwich—everybody just says *chimi*—is pretty much the Dominican Big Mac. The patty is flavored with mad oregano, garlic, and *sazón de adobo.* There is a Thousand Island–like mayo-ketchup on there (which is exactly what it sounds like) and shredded cabbage and sliced onions, and it's served in a paper bag. At La China the roll is kind of panini-ed in the foil wrapper—at the end you should be able to hear the crispness of the bread when you tap it with a fingertip.

ISTED 28. GRILL FLAESKESTEG

First of all, you're not going to think Isted Grill has anything good in there—it's a little shithole, a little grease-bucket spot in Copenhagen run by a Chinese couple everybody calls Mr. and Mrs. Lee. But I'll eat anything from there: the burger, the Belgian-style fries, both amazing. And their *flaeskesteg*—that sandwich is top five for me. Flaeskesteg is the Danish version of roast pork. Mr. Lee gets pork loin or some similar cut with the skin still on and roasts that thing till the outer edge gets all crackly. Then he slices it and fries it again on his flattop. The sandwich gets Danish purple cabbage stewed with vinegar, some sliced cucumber pickles, and a perfect sesame-seeded hamburger bun. I asked Mr. Lee to put a little mayo and a little mustard on mine, which is not traditional—he usually makes it with *rémoulade* sauce, but I don't like that. We went back many times to Isted Grill on our last trip, because this sandwich was crack. It's also just a scene there at night: Isted Grill serves food for drunk people. As soon as we walked in the first time, a guy started poking me in the stomach and touching my beard. I wanted to beat the shit out of him, but I wanted a sandwich more.

29.

THE BUTCHER SANDWICH

The butcher sandwich
a guy like me would eat.

SERVES 2

At Eataly in Manhattan you can get an amazing butcher sandwich. Just shaved, roasted rib eye with extra virgin olive oil and sea salt on an Italian roll—that's it. I love that version, but then I went to Gjusta in Venice, in L.A. On their butcher sandwich—they have an incredible flesh program and a dope bakery—they hand-cut the meat for me a little thicker, which gives it a slightly different taste. Instead of an Italian roll, it was a heartier sourdough loaf, and of course because I always have to kick it up a notch, they also shaved horseradish on it. I came home and made my own version, using a fucking beautiful grass-fed rib eye, Calabrian chile paste, tart ricotta salata, fresh basil, and the funky, sweet *Madre de Sagrantino* (page 185), which is the sludge, the remnants of what was left over in the barrel from making a natural Sagrantino wine at Paolo Bea winery in Italy. It looks like you just changed the oil from a fucking Chevy Celebrity. You can mimic the flavor by cooking down Concord grape jam with a funky natural red wine and use that instead of the madre. Then you get to drink the wine while you make the steak.

¼ cup (60 ml) Concord grape jam
1½ teaspoons red wine (preferably a natural wine, such as Sagrantino from Paolo Bea winery)
Dash of good-quality red wine vinegar
1 (1-pound/455-g) boneless rib eye steak
Flaky sea salt
Extra virgin olive oil (decent, for cooking)
1 foot-long (30.5-cm) sesame seeded semolina sub roll
Softened butter, optional
2 to 3 tablespoons Calabrian chile paste
4 ounces (115 g) ricotta salata
Extra virgin olive oil (amazing, for finishing)
1 small stem fresh basil

1. In a small saucepan, whisk the jam over very low heat until it is smooth and melted. Turn off the heat and whisk in the wine and the vinegar. This is your mimic of the madre de Sagrantino, though you know it won't be exactly the same. Set aside to cool while you make the steak.

2. Heat a cast-iron skillet over medium-high heat until it is roaring hot, about 10 minutes.

3. Salt the rib eye freely on both sides and drizzle one side with the decent olive oil. Place the oiled side facedown in the hot skillet, making sure the steak is pressed flat against the pan. It will smoke. It will set off the fire alarm.

4. Let it cook for 3 to 4 minutes without moving it, or until the bottom is black-brown and crusty-crunchy. It's all about almost burning it—that's where you get that mad flavor from. Then drizzle on a little of the decent oil and use tongs to flip it over.

5. Cook the steak without moving it for 3 to 4 minutes more, until the other side is black-brown and crusty, then remove it to a cutting board. You want it medium-rare, pink, and gorgeous on the inside, which is exactly what it will be.

6. Now you drink a glass of wine while you wait for the steak to rest, at least 10 minutes. Then slice it up, across the grain, into nice big cuts about ¼ inch (6 mm) thick.

7. Slice the roll in half lengthwise. Here I like to smear the outside with butter and toast it in the hot steak fat in the pan, and I put a tablespoon or two of butter on top of the steak as it rests, just for extra flavor.

8. Smear the bottom with your mimic madre and the top half with the chile paste.

9. Add the steak slices to the bottom of the loaf. Use a vegetable peeler to shave a good amount of ricotta salata directly over the slices (you won't use all of it, unless you want to), then douse it with the amazing olive oil, enough so it drips off and starts to soak into the bread. Tear the basil leaves over the top, and sprinkle on a little more salt and oil. Close and eat.

30

D'ANGELO'S SAUSAGE AND PEPPERS

D'Angelo's Italian Sausage & Heros is a truck always parked outside the cemetery on Woodhaven Boulevard in Queens. Their sausage and peppers is one of the city's major sandwiches—I get it special with the mustard *and* the peppers and onions, and I go hot with a little bit of sweet sausage on top too. This place is obviously a legend in the neighborhood—everybody's known since 1973—but I didn't know that till after I'd had it.

31.

THE FALAFEL FROM GRILL POINT

Grill Point is on the part of Main Street in Queens that we called Jewish Main Street, because that part is in a Hasidic neighborhood. Then there's the other part of Main Street in the center of Flushing, where all the stores are Asian. They're Israeli at Grill Point, which is usually my favorite form of falafel. I've had the Egyptian version, the Tunisian version, the Persian version—they're cool, but they're totally different. Grill Point's is what I like: I like to be able to taste all the chickpea coarseness in there, I like to be able to taste all the garlic and herbaceousness and other beautiful stuff in there. It's perfectly salted and cooked through the middle, and they put French fries in the sandwich and let you pick your own pickles from the salad bar. The pita is also that fluffy, white, beautiful kind of pita, not the Sahara pita bread in the orange packets. My mother would always buy that packaged shit and she would use it to make tuna sandwiches. The smell of that pita is just etched in my mind in a bad way. So is the tuna fish. Tuna fish was a big thing in my house, because my mother was a Brooklyn Jew who grew up in the forties just after the Depression—you'll never go hungry if you have canned tuna. There was only one kind in the house—Bumble Bee. Never the StarKist. And it would always be packed in water, and it was disgusting, especially with that pita.

PASTRAMI

I grew up going to amazing Jewish delis like Ben's Best in Queens—which has the best French fries in the history of life, a fat crinkle cut, they're crazy—or the ones my grandfather would take us to in West Palm Beach, Florida. But the best pastrami sandwich I have ever had was at SkyCity Casino in Auckland, New Zealand. It has a Jewish deli on the first floor called Federal Delicatessen. The pastrami there is really smoked meat, the Montreal version of pastrami—both are cured, smoked, steamed beef, but with a slightly different cut, a slightly different seasoning. At Federal the smoked meat is Chef Al Brown's version of what they do in Montreal, where he worked for years, but it's really his own thing, because of the mānuka wood that they use to smoke things in New Zealand. That wood does something that's magical—it gives the best flavor I've ever had on anything smoked.

33. FIG AND ROBIOLA ON CIABATTA

Cherry Valley is a deli I used to go to back in the day—they have about fifty different sandwiches, and everyone in Queens knew about it somehow. No matter what Body and I did, at the end of the night around two in the morning, we would look at each other and go, *Yo—Cherry Valley?* Boom, boom, boom—thirty minutes later we're eating sandwiches on the hood of the car. The sandwich I used to get from there all the time was called the Lean Boy, but there was nothing really lean about it: It was honey turkey, mozzarella cheese, gravy, and sautéed onions. It was not a popular sandwich, but it was fire. Now we have moved on down the block to Tony's Beechhurst, which is a staple in the Whitestone area of Queens. Everyone knows about it, everyone loves it. They do sandwiches and beautiful prepared foods. There my thing is my own creation: Fig preserves and soft Italian robiola cheese on toasted ciabatta with olive oil.

34. THE LIVERACCE

Philly is a sandwich town. Of course there is the Philly cheesesteak, and I do love a classic cheesesteak—I have had them at almost every place: Tony Luke's, Pat's, Geno's, Ishkabibbles, Jim's on South Street, new start-ups, little niche places, this place, that place. However, I feel like all cheesesteaks* can start to taste the same, and one of the best places in Philly for all the other kinds of sandwiches is Paesano's Philly Style, run by Chef Peter McAndrews. He makes a good sausage and peppers, a meatloaf Parm, an Italian cold cut, and all kinds of other good sandwiches, but the Liveracce hoagie was one of the craziest flavors I have ever tasted. That sandwich! It's a real eater's sandwich: A novice is not going to go in there and order that sandwich. It's got bright orange, buffalo-style spicy fried chicken livers, gorgonzola sauce, fried imported Italian salami, shredded iceberg lettuce, roasted tomatoes, and garlic mayo. And when I was there, Chef also added orange marmalade and banana peppers, then wrapped it all up nice and tight. I was like, *What the fuck are you doing, you prick?* It was so good, I was angry at him. This is a one-bite sandwich, as it eats like a bag of nickels to the face. As in take a bite, pass it on.

 I like my Philly cheesesteak with onions and with provolone. I mean, I'll eat it with Whiz, but I like the provolone much better, and I also love to dip it in ketchup. I don't care what anyone says.

BACON CHICHARRÓN ON WHITE BREAD

Fringe the fat.

MAKES AT LEAST 4 SANDWICHES

I like to cook thick slices of maple-smoked bacon as if it were Colombian *chicharrón*, which is pork belly that's been fringed before it's fried. I just cut the slices so they look like a comb, then fry them in their own fat. You serve it on buttered white bread with pickles, or you could just pull off the individual bites and eat it with onion and tomato in the style of Peter Luger Steak House.

2 pounds (1 kg) unsliced maple-smoked bacon
8 slices white bread
Unsalted butter, softened
Pickle slices

1. Cut the bacon crosswise into 16 slices about 1 inch (2.5 cm) thick.

2. Cut a fringe along the bottom of each slice about ½ inch (12 mm) apart, so that the bacon slice looks like a comb.

3. Heat a large cast-iron skillet over medium to high heat, and lay the slices evenly in the pan. Let them fry for at least 10 minutes—I like to let them go until they are caramelized and brown and all the fat gets crunched, even in between the toes. Remove to paper towels. You may need to cook them in batches, and you may want to drain some of the fat off from time to time. (You can use it for other things, as in cook some onions in the bitch.)

4. When all the bacon is fried, lightly brush one side of the bread slices with the butter and press the buttered side of each slice into the hot pan until just softened.

5. Prepare each sandwich with 3 to 4 slices of fried bacon and a few pickle slices.

36. THE PINBONE FRIED CHICKEN PANINI

Just bizarrely good.

SERVES 6

I had a perfect fried chicken sandwich in Australia at a Sydney restaurant called 10 William St. I was in a little romantic corner with Meyhem, drinking a lot of Susucaru, my favorite from Mt. Etna. Jemma Whiteman and Mike Eggert, who run the natural wine–friendly restaurant Pinbone, were in the kitchen—they were doing a takeover because their first spot had to close. They made all kinds of approachable but edgy Italian kind of shit—smoked whipped *bottarga* with a pretzel, lamb ragù pappardelle—but this sandwich, that's what I still talk about. The chicken had a super-crunchy crust, but the bread is what made it. They call it panini, but it's really on a milk bun, which is kind of an Asian thing, that shiny round thing you get from Chinese bakeries that looks like a hamburger bun but is softer and a little sweeter. Apparently they are to Australia what Martin's Potato Rolls are to us—the thing everybody cool puts their hamburger on. That was a special sandwich, because they also butter and toast that bun, they fry the chicken twice, they use two flours in the batter, they make a special hot sauce, and they smoke their own cheese—all those steps matter. This recipe is directly from them.

FOR THE MARINADE AND CHICKEN
1 quart (1 L) buttermilk
¾ cup (150 g) superfine sugar
¼ cup (75 g) fine salt
6 boneless, skinless chicken thigh fillets, pounded to an even thinness (see **NOTE**)

FOR THE JALAPEÑO HOT SAUCE
1 tablespoon vegetable oil
8 ounces (200 g) jalapeño chiles, stemmed and roughly chopped
2 small yellow onions, sliced
8 cloves garlic, crushed

½ cup (120 ml) rice vinegar
¼ cup (50 g) packed dark brown sugar
Salt

FOR THE DREDGE AND FRY
2 to 3 quarts (2 to 3 L) vegetable oil
1½ cups (220 g) rice flour
2 cups (250 g) cornstarch

FOR THE PANINI
2 tablespoons unsalted butter
6 Chinese milk buns or other soft hamburger buns
Mayonnaise
12 slices smoked Gouda or another smoked cheese
6 tomato slices
6 pieces green oakleaf lettuce

1. Make the marinade: Whisk together the buttermilk, sugar, and salt in a large bowl. Place the chicken thighs in the marinade, making sure they are fully coated. Cover and refrigerate for at least 4 hours and up to 8.

2. Make the hot sauce: Heat the oil in a large skillet over medium-low heat and add the chiles, onions, and garlic. Cook, stirring occasionally, for about 20 minutes, until the chiles start to soften—you don't want anything to brown, just soften. (Chefs calls this sweating.)

3. Add the vinegar and sugar, reduce the heat to low, and let the chiles and onions cook until they are very soft, another 15 to 20 minutes.

4. While they're still warm, zap them in the food processor with a pinch of salt until smooth. Taste for salt, adding more if you like. This makes about 2 cups (500 ml). Set aside or refrigerate—just bring it up to room temp before you use it.

5. To fry the chicken, fill a Dutch oven or heavy-bottomed stockpot about halfway up the sides with vegetable oil. Heat the oil over high heat to about 320°F (160°C). Place a wire rack over a baking sheet.

6. Mix the rice flour and cornstarch in a large bowl. Remove the chicken from the marinade and dredge each piece completely in the flour mixture. Shake off the excess flour and set the chicken pieces aside on another baking sheet or large plate.

7. Fry the chicken thighs in batches—they shouldn't touch—in the pot for 4 minutes, then allow them to cool completely on the wire rack. Fry them again at 360°F (180°C) for 2 minutes, then set them back on the rack while you assemble the panini.

8. To make the sandwiches: Melt the butter in a large skillet over medium heat until it just begins to sizzle. Place the buns facedown in the skillet and toast until golden brown, about 2 minutes.

9. Spread the bottom halves of the buns with mayonnaise and the tops with the jalapeño hot sauce. Lay a piece of cheese on the bottom, then add a chicken thigh and another piece of cheese. Top with a slice of tomato and a piece of lettuce. Finish with the top bun. Serve immediately.

NOTE: You can ask your butcher to make the thigh fillets, which is the easy way, or you can do your own from boneless, skinless chicken thighs. Unroll them; trim off the odd bits and extra skin; pound them pretty thin, about ¼ inch (6 cm); trim them into sandwich-size fillets. Then fry the odd bits to eat later too. You can usually get 6 fillets from 4 or 5 thighs.

37. BBQ TURKEY FOLDIE

LocoL is Chefs Daniel Patterson and Roy Choi's fast-food spot in the Los Angeles neighborhood of Watts, where they're trying to do better fast food. They make this little turkey taco–melt type of thing in a thick homemade corn tortilla. Roy calls it a BBQ turkey foldie, and it is a fucking sick combination of flavors: barbecue sauce, some cheddar, sliced turkey breast. You put the whole thing on the griddle until it gets melty and melded. I feel like he added this sandwich to this spot because everyone in the hood knows the turkey foldie: You get some cold cuts at the store—some turkey, some American cheese—you fold them in a flour tortilla, you pop it in the Foreman grill, and you have a turkey foldie. Roy took it to the next level: He added barbecue sauce, he made his own tortilla. This is something that is near and dear to many people's hearts, because you could also make it for yourself after school. Which is why George Foreman is the legend he is today— not because he was a great boxer, but because of the grill, the most incredible invention of the past thirty years.

Power light that goes green when it's ready

Plastic grill comb that cleans perfectly

Grates that heat from both sides

Hinges so it folds flat

Drip tray for the fat

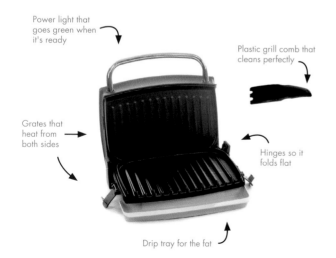

38. AN OCTOPUS SANDWICH

Octopus on bread is not typical, but it is amazing. In Barcelona, I ate at Bobo Pulpín from the famous Iglesias brothers out there—*pulpo* means octopus, which I tell you all about on page 142—where I had Peruvian-style fried octopus on black squid-ink bread with chopped tomatoes and onions. The other octopus sandwich I have been dreaming about is from one of the most amazing human beings I have ever met in my life: Tom, this older guy in Australia who owned an Italian deli called Di Chiera Brothers. His family is originally from Italy—they all came to Perth years ago. He was also into rockabilly, and we drove around in this gold-topped Cadillac DeVille that he has. He was making me all his sandwiches, but when I saw he also had this octopus salad, essentially just charred octopus and oil, I said, *Why don't you just fucking put this on a sandwich?* He added roasted red peppers, some spicy Caprese salami, and some pickled Calabrese chiles and put it on this nice, home-baked Italian bread. Now that shit was fire. ●

To the right is me and Yoda (see page 215) in Perth, pondering our lives and looking for pigface, which is a slimy, salty, fig-strawberry type of thing that grows wild on the coast right on the sand dunes in western Australia. Below is Meyhem, knee-deep in the shark-infested waters of the Indian Ocean, which he was too petrified to swim. This is a known area for bull sharks, where I was diving for clam-like substances. Everything else, Di Chiera Brothers from page 101.

39. EGGS AND PEPPERS

The eggs just gently soft.

SERVES 1

Eggs and peppers is an Albanian peasant dish we had for breakfast all the time. There's a technique to it. You fry the peppers first in a little oil—and make sure that you have either the long hots or Anaheim—until they're blistered on both sides. Then you just crack the eggs on top of them, breaking the yolks gently between the holes in the peppers with a wooden spoon, and let them cook with the residual heat. The eggs form this marbling of yolk and white that's just softly stirred together, and then you top them with very beautiful pieces of Maldon sea salt, excuse me very much. My kicked-up version these days is to leave out the peppers and hit it with a little bit of olive oil and throw white truffle all over the top, or right at the end stir in a little Madre de Sagrantino like from page 185, excuse me very much.

Extra virgin olive oil
3 long straight peppers, preferably long hots or Anaheim
Flaky sea salt
3 large eggs

1. Over medium-high heat, add olive oil to coat the bottom of a medium skillet. Add the peppers to the pan—if they stick out a little, it will be fine—and sprinkle them with sea salt. Leave them be and let them fry until one side starts to blister and soften—a minute or two—then flip them over and do the same on all other sides until they are soft and browned. Spatter will happen. It's OK.

2. When the peppers are soft, add the eggs to the pan one at a time, dropping them in between the peppers where they fit. Break the yolks with a wooden spoon very gently, moving them a little with the spoon so the egg fills in any holes around the peppers and the entire pan is a complete circle of eggs and peppers. (If you're making it without peppers, just fill in the circle with eggs.)

3. Let it cook for a minute or two on low, low, low heat—the lowest possible heat, which sometimes means taking it off the eye if it looks like the egg is cooking too quickly. You never want these to get fried or too brown. When the eggs are beginning to set but the white is still loose and Jell-O-y, turn off the heat and let them sit for about 3 to 5 minutes. They will continue to cook in the pan and come out perfectly. In fact, this is even better when it sits out a little.

4. Sprinkle on a little more salt and scoop up the eggs and peppers with bread.

THE ART OF SCARPETTA

Scarpetta is an Italian term for reseasoning what's left in the pan. You just luxurize it by rehitting it with a little extra something, then you lap it up. Massimo Bottura taught me the word—all my life it's been going down right in front of my eyes and it took an Italian guy to tell me what it was called. My nonna would always wait until everyone had eaten, and then she would schlop up everything left with a little bit of salt and olive oil. That's an art right there.

CHARRED PEPPERS

I don't really love salad. What I love are vegetables charred on the grill. At the nice Turkish kebab spot, the roasted pepper from the grill is my favorite thing. My nonna would shop for peppers at Aron's Kissena Farms, a kosher supermarket near our house, and she would only buy straight ones, never the curly ones, because the straight ones work better. At the Turkish place they bring them straight from the grill, but I like to char them directly over the electric or gas eye of the stove until they are blackened all over, then put them to steam in a plastic bag—like the one you put them in at the grocery store—so they soften.

MADRE DE
SAGRANTINO

TRUFFLES

PEPPERS

When I worked in the kitchen of my father's place, we had a little TV on top of the fridge and I would watch PBS constantly: Ming Tsai, Rick Bayless, and Martin Yan*—I fucking love them all, but Jacques Pépin was my fucking guy right there. He's the god. He's just ill—he's an OG, like watching Al Green sing. Jacques is just this old classy Frenchman, like your French grandfather who goes wild in the kitchen and wants to make you happy with food. Watching him in the kitchen by himself and with Julia Child inspired me to try a lot of different things. Once he made fried Camembert on a Nicoise salad on TV and I made it as a special at the restaurant where I was working right away: You put herbes de Provence in the fry batter, then the fried cheese goes on top of the salad with a little Dijon mustard–lemon type of dressing. It was a special in my stomach—and I also did it for a couple of bar customers who were always there.

Jacques Pépin

 Also don't forget Emeril and Mario, who really made me want to be on TV cooking, and Bourdain and Zimmern, who just made food on TV look extra cool. Zimmern made it look weird and cool. And Bayless taught me how to make *cochinita pibil.*

Chipwich

At the beach when I was growing up, me and my cousins would always get ice cream from the carts, like Fudgie Wudgie bars and Chipwich. (My cousins used to call me Fudgie Wudgie because I was fat, but I would always get the Chipwich.) The Chipwich ice cream cookie sandwich was invented in 1981 right in Queens, and there's no doubt about it—it was one of life's perfections. Even to this day, I am definitely a sucker for ice cream in between two cookies. There are also the Toll House chocolate chip cookie ice cream sandwiches by Nestlé. The Toll House versions are good, but they could never be the Chipwich, which is more compact and has the chips on the outside of the ice cream instead of inside.

42. My Momma's Challah

It's really fucking special.

MAKES 2 NICE BIG ONES

My momma says: "I found this recipe in a book years ago, but as I keep making it I do my thing. I went through hundreds of recipes, and to me this one is the best. I just love to make challah, I love to work the dough, and I know it's going to come out good, because it always does if you love making something. You can freeze the dough at any stage before baking, then just bring it to room temperature, and you can make several smaller loaves instead of two large ones. I used to add a little vanilla, which was a more Middle Eastern recipe from Latvia. I also only use Heckers flour—my mother-in-law only used this flour, and after years of making challah I can tell you there really is a difference. You're supposed to let it cool before eating it, but I usually go right in, because how can you not?"

5 large eggs

2 (¼-ounce / 7-g) packages active dry yeast

½ cup (100 g) sugar

1 heaping tablespoon table salt

7 cups (875 g) all-purpose flour, plus extra for dusting

½ cup (120 ml) canola oil, plus extra for greasing the bowl

1¾ cups (420 ml) lukewarm water

Flaky sea salt

1. In a medium bowl, beat 4 of the eggs. In your largest mixing bowl, whisk together the yeast, sugar, and salt. Stir in 2 cups (250 g) of the flour. Then add the oil, the beaten eggs, and the water and stir with a wooden spoon until incorporated.

2. Stir in remaining 5 cups (625 g) flour slowly, working it in 1 cup (125 g) at a time. When it gets too tight to stir with the spoon, use floured hands to work it together in the bowl. When the dough is not wet anymore but still sticky, dump the contents of the bowl onto a clean floured work surface.

3. Knead the dough by folding it back over on itself repeatedly until it feels smooth, silky, shiny, and very soft. Sprinkle on a little more flour as you knead if the dough is still sticky. This may take several minutes, so be patient: The key is not kneading it for a certain time but to keep going until it feels soft and smooth.

4. Form the dough into a loose ball. Coat all sides of a clean mixing bowl with a light coating of oil. Place the dough ball in the bowl and turn it so all sides get coated in oil, then cover the bowl loosely with plastic wrap or a supermarket shopping bag as described on page 38.

5. Let the dough rise until it is doubled in size, usually at least 1 hour and sometimes several—you can't be in a rush to make challah. Make a fist and punch it down, then let it rise again.

6. When the dough has risen again to where you can't see the imprint of your hand anymore, punch it down again and then form the loaves.

7. Sprinkle flour onto a clean work surface, roll the dough into a fat rectangular link, and divide it into 6 equal pieces. With your hands, roll each piece—start in the middle and work out—into a rope about 15 inches (38 cm) long.

8. Line a large baking sheet with parchment paper.

9. To make one loaf, take 3 of the pieces of dough and braid them together. It's easier to start the braid in the middle of the ropes, so you don't end up with one end tighter than the other. If the dough is hard to stretch, let it sit for about 10 minutes and it will relax a bit. When you're

done, pinch the ends together and turn the pinched parts under the loaf.

10. Repeat the process with the remaining 3 pieces of dough. (If you want, you can take a little dough from each of the pieces and make a small decorative braid to place on top of the challah, just pinch it on either end.) Place the challahs on the baking sheet.

11. Loosely cover the challahs with plastic wrap and set them aside to rise again, then preheat the oven to 325°F (165°C).

12. When the challahs have almost doubled in size, prepare the egg wash by beating the last egg in a small bowl. Dip a clean kitchen rag or a heavy-duty paper towel in the egg. Holding one edge of the rag or towel, gently drag it over the top of the loaves, using it as a brush, until every surface has been glazed.*

13. Sprinkle on the sea salt and bake for 10 minutes. Increase the heat to 350°F (175°C) and bake for 20 to 30 minutes more, or until they're just golden brown. Let cool a bit before slicing.

* My mother learned this trick by watching them make bagels at Bagel World in West Palm Beach, Florida (see page 29), where we used to go with my grandfather.

43. MARIO BATALI'S OLIVE OIL CAKE

Mario Batali is my food idol. That's who I looked up to coming up—I always wanted to be him. He's so knowledgeable and welcoming and warming and full of ill knowledge—even when he's arrogant, it's cool. *Molto Mario* is my favorite show ever made, and I made a lot of things out of *The Babbo Cookbook*. Then later I ordered those same things at the restaurant sitting next to Mario. The olive oil cake is one of my favorites: It's got a little bit of rosemary, and they top it with an olive oil sorbet with a little lemon hint and brand-new extra virgin olive oil with some sea salt. Usually when we have dinner over there, Rebecca DeAngelis—Babbo's pastry chef—makes as many desserts as people at the table, and Mario makes an announcement: *This is how we do it, fuckers. Taste a little bit, then send it around.* You end up tasting at least seven or eight unbelievable crazy things she's made, but I'm sitting there eyeing the one I really want, watching someone eating it. I'm like, *Yo, move this along.* That cake is like a blunt—you can't wait for it to come back to you. You gotta get at that olive oil cake when you got it, and take that big slop knowing you ain't gonna see it again.

44. JOYCE GOLDSTEIN'S MEDITERRANEAN THE BEAUTIFUL COOKBOOK

This is my favorite cookbook. This thing that has been above the counter in my mother's kitchen in Queens since as long as I can remember, which would be 1994, when it was published. I love this fucking thing: The subtitle is "Authentic Recipes from the Mediterranean Lands," which is my favorite lands, and I also laugh at how big and how weird it is, the long title and how the book is about a foot and a half tall. Joyce Goldstein knows her shit on this region, the source of many of the best flavors in life. Everyone should have this book. You would never see a cookbook published like this now, but I love it. I originally wanted this book to look just like it.

45. PITT CUE

Pitt Cue is a hedonistic farm-to-table barbecue place in London that just blew my fucking socks off. Tom Adams, the chef there, is a young, cool, hip dude doing all these amazing things with these beautiful animals—he and April Bloomfield bought a farm together where they have sheep and Mangalica pigs, and milk cows where the fat is bright yellow. Years ago, a dude brought me a sandwich from Pitt Cue's first spot, a really small place on Carnaby Street. I was mesmerized. Then I went and ate there and met Tom, and it was immediately, *Alright, this guy I love.* Now I go every time I am back in London. My last trip I had bone marrow with demiglace, and mashed potato rye bread soaked in beef drippings and butter that he churned, and short ribs aged for five weeks then smoked, grilled, and basted in mother sauce—all the fat and drippings from his huge grill. I've also had seven-day brined hams, and these amazing beef ribs with a candied caramel coating. I love Tom's cooking, but certain people you connect with—he's a really cool dude. Hey, my heart's an open book.

PITT CUE CARAMEL BEEF RIBS

That candied caramel coating.

SERVES 4

Unless you live in Texas, you're going to have to find a butcher who will cut you a rack of beef back ribs. You can use easier-to-find short ribs in a pinch, though they'll be shorter than what you're really after.

2 racks of beef back ribs, or use short ribs
Salt
¾ cup (190 ml) good-quality cider vinegar
⅓ cup (60 ml) Coca-Cola
1 heaping tablespoon fennel seed
1 heaping tablespoon coriander seed
1 star anise
1 thumb-size knob ginger
1 cup (250 g) sugar
¾ cup (100 g) chipotle in adobo, drained

1. Preheat the oven to 275°F (130°C).

2. Season the ribs with salt and lay them on a rack set into a roasting pan. Roast until just softening, about 1½ hours, or until their internal temperature is 185°F (85°C).

3. Bring the cider vinegar, Coke, spices, and ginger to a boil in a small pot, then turn off the heat and let it sit until the caramel is ready.

4. In a large saucepan, combine the sugar with ½ cup (120 ml) water. Let it simmer over medium-high heat, about 15 minutes, until the sugar syrup reduces and becomes a deep caramel color. As soon as it starts to brown, whisk carefully until it is completed.

5. As soon as the caramel is ready, add the vinegar mixture. Be careful not to stand over it, as the vinegar smell is unpleasant and the mixture may spatter. Rapidly boil this mixture, whisking to blend in all the caramel, for 1 minute, then remove from the heat and let cool.

6. When the caramel has cooled, combine it with the chipotle chiles in a blender and then pass the puree through a sieve. Set aside until needed.

7. Remove the ribs from the oven and turn on the broiler. Cut the ribs apart, place them on a sheet pan, and broil them until they are caramelized and crispy—you could also grill or griddle them.

8. Brush them liberally with the caramel sauce and eat immediately.

JAM

I love Jamaican food: I crave stewed oxtail, I crave jerk chicken, I crave curry chicken. All these things blend techniques and spices and ingredients mixed together in Jamaica over hundreds of years, some from indigenous peoples on the island, some from the Spanish, British, Africans, Indians, and Chinese that moved over and in. It's a gorgeous blend of flavors, and like a lot of New Yorkers, I grew up with them. Half a million Jamaicans live in the city, a lot of them in Queens. So this was a common play for me—just like you go get McDonald's, in Queens you go get Jamaican food. When Meyhem and I finally got to go to Jamaica for the first time—oh, man—that was a life's trip, by which I also mean life-changing. It's one of the most special places I have visited, other than Morocco. We were there mainly to go to Boston Bay, the home of jerk. It's a small town in eastern Jamaica, right on the Caribbean Sea. All these eastern Jamaican towns are crazy rural—you'll be driving, driving, driving through the jungle right along the beachfront. There aren't many roads through the center of this part of Jamaica because that is all Blue Mountains. Then, out of nowhere, you'll suddenly be in a little town, and by town I pretty much mean a few little storefronts—huts, really. We weren't anywhere where you could go to an Old Navy or any chain type of shit. This part of Jamaica was all homegrown, in the real sense. It's a small-size life there—a village.

AICA

Everywhere we were, there was an aura of those Blue Mountains—a high altitude, humongous mountain range. That's where all that crazy good coffee and weed comes from. I don't even drink coffee, and I drank coffee every day in Jamaica because it was so good. No milk: Just black, almost like the way Turkish coffee comes, in the little cups. At that altitude, the weather changes drastically. You have like six different seasons in one day: It'll go from raining unheard of to you can't see an inch in front of you with fog. Then a little bit cold, then it goes to tropical heat. Then it's raining while it's sunny, then uncontrollably windy. It's tropical in the true sense of the word.

In Jamaica, jerk is how you cook food, not just a flavor, and it's not just chicken. Some jerk makers are territorial—they need their own spot to make it all happen—but in Boston Bay we pulled up to a jerk village, where there's all types of people cooking and selling food, including Mickey's Jerk Center, which is where we wanted to go. Mickey had a huge pit going, with a fire in one corner where he was burning wood into charcoal. And then over the other side of the pit, he had laid five different types of fresh wood out across the coals, and they became the grates of the grill: plum wood, laurel, coffee, sweet wood, and then pimento. The food is laid right on top of them. Then he would take four-by-four boards of pimento wood and put them on top of the meat too, and then lay the metal fencing you see in East New York with graffiti on it over the top of all that. That is the flavor of real jerk: The smoke, that wood. The meat itself is also heavily flavored, with spices, scallion, Scotch bonnet peppers, a lot of heat and aromatic flavors you usually find in in sweets, but this is savory. Some of the Jamaican things you eat in New York or Miami or elsewhere are on par with what you can get in Jamaica, but the jerk in Jamaica is just so much better because they have those trees that we don't have growing everywhere.

Mickey had at least five different types of jerk. He had his own slaughterhouse in back, so he had jerk pork sausage, jerk pork neck, jerk lobster, jerk snapper, and jerk conch, which was amazing. Some guy across the road was smoking spicy chicken sausage. All over Jamaica, there's a lot of people on the side of the road with barrel smokers, and you don't know what the fuck's inside them till you get closer: sausage, seafood, pork, chicken, and of course festival. There is festival at every meal in Jamaica and it is always a delight— it's just fried cornmeal dough, but it's like an incredible earthy *zeppole*, crispy and crunchy. You actually gotta work at not eating

117

festival in Jamaica or else you're gonna fucking blow up. Everybody in this jerk village is trying to sell us stuff, whatever they had, yelling at us. Motherfuckers were even pulling up in cabs, running out of the car trying to sell shit to us. They had been called to come through by their friends because we were there. And then out of nowhere, this guy comes up, this Rastaman named Jah Tiger. He was humble: He wasn't asking us for nothing, he wasn't selling us anything. He just wanted to perform his song. So I held his radio for him while he sang "Mr. Two Face." I heard magic. We were dancing. Boom. The next day, I brought him with me to the studio I rented in Jamaica, and we recorded three songs, "Mr. Two Face" being one of them.

It turned out Jah Tiger only ate *ital*. In Rastafarian speak, that means organic and vegetarian. For Jah Tiger it was next-level, real-deal ital. He has to pick his own stuff—he goes foraging in the mountains. A lot of people do that in Jamaica, because you don't have to go far as everything is right there for you: Bananas, passion fruit, plantains, breadfruit, mango—so many kinds of mango. (Some of them are tingly, some of them are stringy, some of them are just straight butter. There's orange ones and there's smaller yellow ones, which tend to be the ones that I go fucking nuts for.) Later on we met up with another ital man named Sazi, who lived in the mountains. His wife was an herbalist, and he would come down from the mountain and cook ital food for people and sell his hot sauce. Sazi walked us through what was growing all around us. He showed us ackee, this creamy fruit that is cooked with salted cod for breakfast in Jamaica. He picked a breadfruit and roasted it right there—he was grilling everything over charcoal stuck inside a 1985 Toyota Corolla tire rim. Then he gave me one of the craziest mind fucks ever, these greens growing wild covered with holes. They were being eaten by the bugs—and Sazi said, *If the insects are not going to eat it, why would I?* That was his mind-set. If the insects don't eat it, it's probably covered with chemicals, pesticides. I don't know why that blew my mind so much, but it was just an amazing perspective. I get it, and I respect it. It's not just food in Jamaica, it is life lessons.

RULES OF ENGAGEMENT

For your first trip to a Jamaican restaurant, you have to get jerk chicken, curry chicken, brown stew chicken, curry vegetables, festival, and the rice and beans. You must, I mean must, get oxtail, which is really usually cow tails stewed and stewed until they are unbelievably tender and delicious and become the single most decadent thing in the world after foie gras and bone marrow, like you've been drinking fat mixed with pot roast drippings. I had one piece when I was in Jamaica, and only one, because I knew I wouldn't be able to control myself. Then you must get plantains on the side and at least two different hot sauces—one extremely hot, one a little sweet like the jerk sauce. Usually you will be eating out of foil or Styrofoam in either a seven-dollar quantity or a ten-dollar quantity. I usually go for the ten-dollar quantity. If they have the sizes stapled to the wall and the price is written on them in Magic Marker, that's how you know it's real. The other thing you have to know about a Jamaican restaurant is they're going to give you an attitude. Look past that, be extra nice and humble, and warm them up. Or you just have to out-crazy them.

Magical Doughs

FROM THE

Balkans

→

47. GRILLED FLATBREAD with SPICES ON IT

On a trip to my nonna's house in Macedonia a long time ago, we would go out to this restaurant in this little square called Turista, which made the Balkan *cevapi* (see page 72) and *pasul* (see page 54) and all this other traditional stuff. These guys made bread, and they would put oil on top and grill it but sprinkle something on the bread first to make it taste unbelievable. When I got back home, I would be making these little pizzas with leftover grilled flatbread. I would do a tomato-mozzarella-basil one; a Hawaiian one with some of the *salsa macha* from page 183; some country French smoked ham, pineapple, and white cheddar; or mushrooms with black pepper, Taleggio cheese, and sautéed onions.

Today I make the one on page 122 with ricotta, hazelnuts, and jalapeño honey. But I would often just add olive oil, salt, pepper, and this homemade *zaatar* powder that I make—it's just sesame seeds and thyme and some chile flakes and garlic powder. I would put the pita in a frying pan with a little oil to crisp up the bottom, then I'd run it under the broiler. I was really trying to mimic the bread I had in Macedonia. I'd try it with all different spice sprinkles, but I never got it right.

Years later, I was at my boy Toastie's house in Toronto. He's a guy in the cannabis community. He's half-Serbian, and usually Albanians wouldn't be at somebody Serbian's house, but this fucking kid is a nice guy. When I went over, he got out some foods from the land to welcome me—cevapi, desserts, and different breads. I watched as he did this technique where he took the thick Balkan pita bread, dunked it very lightly in soup made with Vegeta, this Balkan spice mix, then put it back on the grill. It was just like that bread from Macedonia. It's just crazy that after all these years of searching, the technique was at a dabber's house in Toronto. It fucking blew my mind.

GRILLED BALKAN BREAD WITH VEGETA SOUP FLAVOR

1. Make a small pot of chicken soup and season it with Vegeta until it tastes amazing.

2. Get a stack of Bosnian, Serbian, Albanian, Croatian, or other Balkan flatbread, what people sometimes call *lepinja* or *somun*. If you can't find it, very thick pita—like the homemade kind—is your substitute.

3. Use tongs to quickly dunk the bread into the soup. Drizzle extra virgin olive oil all over the bread—you can do this right over the soup pot—and then grill or char it in some other way, such as over the eye of your stove or in your broiler. Cook a few minutes on both sides, being gentle as you flip. The real goal here is to slightly char it, turning often so it doesn't really burn (or totally catch fire, if it's your stovetop).

4. When the breads are charred, carefully dunk them in the Vegeta soup again, then add them to the platter. Drizzle them with more olive oil, sprinkle them with sea salt, and serve right away with good yogurt or grilled meats.

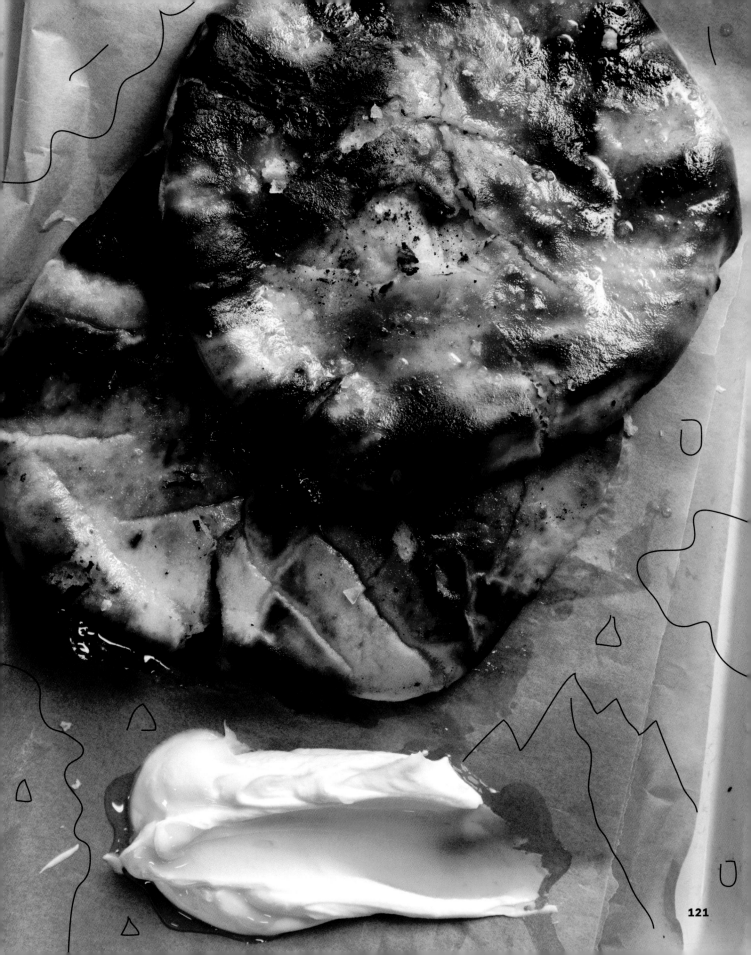

FLATBREADS *with* RICOTTA *and* PICKLED JALAPEÑO HONEY

Olive oil before, during, and after.

MAKES 4 FLATBREAD PIZZAS

This started as a Neapolitan-style pie I made for myself at my birthday party at Otto, but it is also banging as a flatbread pizza on leftover Balkan bread like the ones on the previous page. I like to use La Morena pickled jalapeños as they have a good kick to them. Pair it with a ginger ale.

1 12 ounce (340 g) bear of clover honey
3 pickled jalapeños, diced
Calabrian chile oil, optional
4 Balkan flatbreads or thick pitas
Extra virgin olive oil
8 ounces (245 g) good-quality ricotta cheese
1 cup (135 g) hazelnuts

1. Preheat your broiler and set out a sheet pan.

2. In a small mixing bowl, stir together the clover honey and the pickled jalapeños. If you want, swirl in a little Calabrian chile oil for color too. Set aside.

3. Drizzle a little olive oil over the top of the breads, then spread each with ¼ of the ricotta cheese and sprinkle on ¼ of the hazelnuts. Place them on a baking sheet and drizzle them with olive oil again.

4. Coat the bottom of a small skillet with olive oil, then heat it over medium-high. Add one of the flatbread pizzas and cook just until the bottom has toasted. Remove it to the sheet pan and repeat with the remaining 3 pies.

5. Toast the pies under the broiler until the edges of the bread and the top of the hazelnuts are well toasted. Drizzle on some of the pickled chile-honey (you'll have some left over, but it keeps forever), then some more olive oil, and eat right away.

48. PETLA

Petla is every child's dream. It is an Albanian-style sweet fried yeast dough my nonna always made, just like Italian *zeppole* but without powdered sugar and in more free-form shapes, just thrown into the hot oil. I saw her make mad petla when my cousin got married in Macedonia about a decade ago—they told me for a wedding you usually bring petla. My grandmother was the matriarch of the family, and all the ladies would come over and help her out. She sets up the assembly line of petla making and gets them going. In New York City, fresh zeppole are a big thing at all those Italian-saint street fairs, so I used to get them all the time. They try to put a lot of powdered sugar on them, but being that I was familiar with petla, I would always ask for my zeppole without sugar. All the Italian guys would look at me like, *Ohh, you know.* Like I was a part of this purist club of those seeking fried dough bliss. Coincidentally, I also used to work in a zeppole stand when I was around thirteen, run by an old man in the building over from mine. I got twenty dollars for each twelve-hour day. I was tight—that's not enough money for all day long. The lesson I learned: Don't let anybody overwork you for a little bit of fucking money, but I also learned how to work hard. Honestly, the moral of the story is: You work hard, for a long time, and eventually you own your own zeppole stand.

ACTION: My relatives used to call me *petla.* Also, my Albanian uncle, he called me *chombay*.
RACHEL: What does chombay mean?
ACTION: I don't know, but I am sure it has something to do with being husky—it just sounds that way.

MOMMA'S PITE WITH CHEESE

My mother also makes a version of a butter-soaked, feta-stuffed Albanian pastry we call *pite*, which is also known as *burek*. She fills it with egg and feta, but you can make meat or spinach pite too. My mother's version of cheese pite or burek is totally different from the one my Albanian relatives make, and to me it's better. She gets the crunch. It's a different shape, a horseshoe rather than a coil or a pie, and really she doesn't do anything right. She freezes the dough and lowers the temperature a hundred degrees midway through, then flips them and bastes them with butter half a dozen times, taking them out of the oven every time. A baker would be like, *That's not how you do it, you can't do that.* But the technique just works, and now I crave it. I even love it when it's cold, with some ketchup on it in the middle of the night. My mother makes it with a certain hand: My grandmother used to have the hand when she made it, and now my mother has the hand.

49. KERLANA

Kerlana is unreal—where this recipe came from is beyond me, how anyone ever thought to do this. It's twice-baked dough with butter and feta. My nonna would mix up a very wet dough, like a thick pancake batter, and she would spread it out in a rectangular glass baking dish, a Pyrex-type thing. She would bake it halfway, to where it was cooked around the edges but still raw inside. While it was still hot as a motherfucker, she would hollow out the bread, digging out the dough with her hands and ripping it into little pieces. One of the things I would have to do when she made it was just eat that half-raw dough right as she would be ripping it out. Then she piled all those pieces of raw dough back in the middle of the pan and drizzled butter all over it before she put it back in the oven. And then five minutes before it was done, she added feta cheese to that, mixed it in, and then a little more feta on top after it was done. You would end up with this crunchy, crispy, buttery shell on the bottom that acted like a vessel—like the bottom of a boat filled with all those incredible little ripped-up balls of dough soaked in butter and feta cheese. The best part is getting that crunchy shell mixed with the soft insides. For a long time, I thought my grandmother invented this, because I'd never heard of anyone else who knew about it. There's nothing like it—I miss that dish in my life, but it's some ancient secret I don't know.

There's also *flija*, which is the most handcrafted thing—it requires technical fucking mastery to make that dish. It's wizardry, a very special dish for the holidays. It's a loose pancake batter, like a crepe. You layer it over a hot pan in a hot oven, leaving spaces that you fill in as it bakes. And you keep filling in and baking for thirty layers, until it becomes this flaky piece of dough. I learned how from my grandmother—I went over there and learned how to do all those things she used to make. I wrote down all her recipes in a book, but I don't know where it is—maybe in my mother's house somewhere. It would be priceless if I could find it. ●

50. LAHORE KEBAB HOUSE

As soon as we touch down in London, it's usually Lahore time. A little curry and burning flesh spiced very expensively gets you over your jet lag, like you took a little bump of fucking cumin. Lahore is a magical fucking place, with lamb chops that legends are made of. It is my Pakistani food temple, mainly for those lamb chops: Every single time they blow my mind. Sliced thin, still on the bone, smeared with Punjabi spices and cooked over the flames—the whole kitchen is just skewers of charred meats and big pots sitting right in the fire. In everything here you taste that fire. I also get *seekh kebab*—long kebabs of chopped lamb with crazy spices, and they do a great lamb vindaloo, spicy as a motherfucker. I always get the vegetable masala, the curry vegetables, and the chicken saag—the one with the spinach curry—the chana masala, or curried chickpeas, for sure. Plus buttered naan and the plate of cucumbers, lettuce, and whole green chiles they always give you. Every time I order lamb chops at a Pakistani place anywhere else I have this feeling, this hope, that they're going to be made in this way, and they're not.

51. LA KALADA SMOKERS CLUB

In Barcelona, I met some young Italian dudes from Abruzzo who run a little social club and are some of the best hash makers ever. Barcelona has a huge cannabis club scene—weed is legal there, but only from these private membership clubs. Anyone can belong, you just have to be cool—meaning they don't want any bullshit in there. At La Kalada, they have a couple of dudes who pay dues to come smoke weed there so they can stay open, and then the owners just get to chill. I had just played the Primavera Sound festival, and I was the only rapper, so I had a huge crowd, and after I did that I made waves in the city. My friend Smoky from London told me these guys wanted me to come see their spot, so I went in: It didn't seem like they were overly excited at first, but then I sit down, and then everyone starts professing their love to me, and they pull out their homemade *porchetta*, the homemade focaccia, the *muzzarelle* that they make in the back, like a proper Italian social club would—like no-joke shit—and a natural wine for me from a producer called Lammidia, also from Abruzzo. We continued to have some of the best times ever had—drinking wine, smoking the unbelievable hash that they make, this pure beautiful shit. The porchetta was also an unbelievable thing, sliced thin, and the Taleggio was just clean-tasting and gorgeous, and then there was the mortadella that they made with pistachios in it. I fucking love mortadella—my favorite thing there was eating that mortadella with the Lammidia. (I also like it cut thick and fried in bread with sweet-sour agrodolce red peppers, like at Salumi, Armandino Batali's place in Seattle.) In fact, making mortadella and making hash is similar: You make it in a big-ass garbage bag with ice to keep the fat cold.

We're in Barcelona, talking about paella theories and of *arroz negro*, which is earthy and deep. Here, I'm in a gorgeous loft in the heart of La Boqueria; top left, in some dude's test kitchen where I made monkfish stew; bottom left, Meyhem eating in slow motion.

52. MY LAMB BURGER

I consider this lamb burger to be one of my original dishes. I am sure lots of people do variations, but this is mine and has been, beginning when I worked at my father's restaurant, where we would run it as a special. He was doing this very regular American burger with cheese, and I figured since it's a Mediterranean restaurant, our customers would be more enamored with something unique. And plus I always had mad time to kill there, just waiting for customers to show up. We used to always just create shit in there—create and eat. I was pretty much using it as my own little test kitchen for my life, my platform. We would make crazy specials—watch Jacques Pépin in the morning, then put whatever he made on the menu that night, or just make up something crazy ourselves. If we didn't have the ingredients lying around, I would literally take money out of the register and go walk down to the C-Town supermarket or go to the Natural World and make sure we had all the good stuff. People loved the shit out of whatever I made.

KOFTA-SPICED LAMB BURGERS WITH GARLIC-YOGURT SAUCE

The scent of heavily spiced lamb always reminds me of home.

SERVES 4

My father was already doing ground lamb *kofta* kebab at his restaurant, which is made all over the Mediterranean—it is *qofte* in Albanian. So I first made the kofta better tasting—you want it to be heavily spiced, a little more coriander-y than cumin-y—and then I turned it into a burger patty with a tzatziki-style sauce on a good piece of fucking bread. These burgers are comfort food to me now.

FOR THE GARLIC-YOGURT SAUCE
1 cup (285 g) thick Greek yogurt
2 cloves garlic, minced
1 heaping tablespoon finely chopped fresh parsley leaves
1 heaping tablespoon finely chopped fresh mint leaves
1 tablespoon fresh lemon juice
¼ cup (40 g) peeled, diced cucumber
Salt

FOR THE BURGERS
1 tablespoon whole coriander seeds
1 teaspoon whole cumin seeds
1 pound (455 g) ground lamb
1 heaping teaspoon red chile flakes
½ teaspoon freshly ground black pepper
Scant ¼ teaspoon ground cinnamon
2 tablespoons finely diced red onion
5 cloves garlic, minced
1 teaspoon salt
Olive oil
4 hamburger buns or large sturdy rolls
4 pieces butter or Bibb lettuce
4 thick slices tomato

1. Make the garlic-yogurt sauce: Stir all the ingredients listed together in a medium bowl, adding salt to taste at the end, then set aside while you make the burgers (see **NOTE**).

2. Next, bloom your spices: We're gonna toast 'em. Put the coriander and cumin seeds whole in a dry skillet over medium heat and stir for 2 to 3 minutes. Do not step away from the pan—they can burn in an instant. (I step away, but only because I am a pro and can smell when it's time to take them off the heat.) When they're done, they should smell amazing—all those essential oils coming out and getting toasty.

3. Remove the spices from the heat to a spice grinder, or mortar and pestle, or some heavy object and a cutting board and roughly crush them. You don't want to pulverize them, you want to keep some rustic chunks in there. I like biting on pieces of coriander seed as I chew the burger.

4. Add the toasted spices to a large stainless steel bowl along with the ground lamb, chile flakes, black pepper, cinnamon, onion, garlic, and salt. If you added a lot of salt to mince your garlic (see below), go lighter on the salt. Mix everything together with your hands until when you pick up a ball of meat and tear it open, the whole thing is studded with spices.

5. Form the meat into 4 patties. You want them to be wider and thinner, not tall and fat. I like to make sure they have very flat bottoms, so that they brown really evenly—but if they don't, it's not the end of the world.

6. Line a paper plate or baking sheet with paper towels. In a large skillet, add just enough olive oil to thinly coat the pan—the slightest

touch, a dribble. Lamb has a lot of fat—this is just so the patties don't stick at first.

7. Heat the pan over medium-high heat—you want it to be real hot, you want those patties to sear.

8. When the oil begins to shimmer, add the patties. They shouldn't touch—you can fry them in batches if you need to. You gotta remember not to fuck with them, either, just flip them once when the bottoms have really browned, 3 to 4 minutes. Then give them another 2 to 3 minutes, until the other side begins to brown too, and remove them to the paper towels. (That's to cook them until almost medium, just barely pink, as I don't like these too rare. You can tell by touching them if you're really good—the meat will have firmed up but will still have some give.)

9. Add the buns to the pan, facedown, and toast them in a little of the hot lamb fat until they're golden brown and a little crispy around the edges.

10. Make the burgers: Yogurt sauce on both sides of the toasted bun, patty on the bottom, then lettuce, tomato. Close, eat.

NOTE: To make the garlic yogurt sauce, I usually just take a whole tub of yogurt and throw in 10 minced garlic cloves, plus one for good luck, at least half a cuke, a fat pinch of herbs, and the juice of one giant lemon. Then I slowly mix it all in with a spoon right in the tub—it's not easy to stir in like that, but I am an artiste and I always make it work—and then I keep the leftovers around to add to the grilled chicken sandwich I get delivered from the diner the next day.

HOW TO PUREE THE SHIT OUT OF GARLIC CLOVES WITH SALT AND A CHEF'S KNIFE

1. A little trick for garlic is to add a little salt, that's how you get it minced. Take your peeled garlics and put them on a large cutting board.

2. Using one hand, hold the flat side of the knife on top of the cloves. Make a fist with your other hand and smash 'em.

3. Roughly mince the crushed cloves and sprinkle them with salt—which becomes

little ball bearings for your knife. I use a large-grained kosher salt, like David's or Diamond Crystal.

4. With the flat side of the knife, crush down and smear the minced, salted bits against the cutting board, working just a few of them at a time, till they become a paste. Smear the shit out of it. It's gonna be perfect, trust me.

LEE TIERNAN'S BEEF-DRIPPING FLATBREAD WITH ONIONS, CHILES, AND PARSLEY

FROM

BLACK AXE MANGAL

One of the best meals I've ever had was in the back of a shitty metal bar in Copenhagen, when London chef Lee Tiernan was running a pop-up called Black Axe Mangal. He was getting Turkish with it—he made all the pita himself, cooking it right on the grill and serving it with smoked lamb shoulder stew, sumac onions, pickled red cabbage, and heirloom tomatoes with parsley leaves, red peppers, and onions. We had just gone to a ton of fucking fancy places, and then we had the best meal of the year in a place with graffiti all over the wall. Lee is the homey—his food was so good we flew him to L.A. a few months later and bought him a mobile smoker so he could make lamb shawarma for the Odd Future Festival, where I sometimes play and make food. (Two years later, the Vice L.A. office shipped me the smoker so I could put it on my balcony and smoke some pork belly with Jamaican jerk powder, but it didn't work, so I had to buy another at the Home Depot.) Black Axe Mangal—*mangal* is the Turkish word for barbecue—is now a real little restaurant in London, where his meats and his flatbreads are the things. It's still like a metal bar in there, though: He smokes all the meats and cooks all his breads in a brick oven painted black with the faces of the four members of KISS on the side.

LEE TIERNAN'S BEEF-DRIPPING FLATBREAD WITH ONIONS, CHILES, AND PARSLEY

Worth it.

MAKES ABOUT 6 CUPS OF BEEF DRIPPINGS

I adapted this recipe by adding a few more cloves of garlic, which I love, and by using pickled capers instead of the anchovies, which I don't like. And I also combined his pickled chiles and marinated red onions into one condiment. Otherwise it's all Lee. At Black Axe Mangal, they pile this mixture onto raw sourdough pizzas and bake it in their brick oven, but it's good on any kind of bread.

FOR THE OXTAILS
2 large oxtails (the fattier the better) cut into pieces
Salt
1 head garlic, cloves separated and peeled
1 small bunch thyme
1 can IPA or stout beer

FOR THE FLATBREADS
2 long red chiles
2 purple onions, thinly sliced
Juice from 4 limes
Good-quality extra virgin olive oil
Salt
6 flatbreads
Salted capers, rinsed
1 medium bunch parsley, leaves only

1. In a large mixing bowl or ziplock bag, season the oxtails liberally with salt. Toss the meat with the garlic and thyme, pour in the beer, and store overnight in the fridge. Alternatively, you can leave it out of the fridge for 4 or so hours if you're planning on cooking it the same day.

2. Preheat your oven to 400°F (205°C).

3. Place the oxtails, garlic, thyme, and beer into an oven-proof dish or pot. The meat should be pretty snug, and the pot should be deep enough to facilitate the liquid plus whatever fat renders out of the tails.

4. Cover the dish with parchment paper and a very tight "lid" of foil. (Says Lee, "If you double over the foil it will be more obedient and give you a tighter seal. It's important for the tails to steam, so a tight seal is imperative.")

5. Put the oxtails in the oven for 1 hour, then lower the heat to 230°F (110°C). Cook for 7 to 8 hours, or until the meat parts with the bone with no resistance. Let it cool until you can handle the tails comfortably without burning your hands. Pull all the meat from the bones, discarding the bones and bits and thyme twigs, gently shredding the meat and pureeing the garlic cloves into the liquid. (Says Lee: "Don't mulch the meat too much as we want to avoid all your hard work turning into corned beef.")

6. Taste for seasoning, adding salt if necessary, then place the mixture into a plastic container with a lid. Refrigerate until it is fully chilled and the fat is jellified and binds everything together. This can last for a week in the fridge. (You'll probably have extra left over.)

7. When you're ready to make the flatbreads, prepare the chiles and parsley: Char the chiles on the stovetop or the broiler, then chop them into rounds. In a small bowl, mix the charred chiles, the onions, the lime juice, a drizzle of olive oil, and a pinch of salt. Taste for seasoning and set aside to marinate.

8. Preheat your broiler.

9. Use a spoon to spread the flatbreads with some of the beef drippings mixture, being careful not to lay it on too thick or it won't heat up as well. (Says Lee: "There is no pretty way to put this on the bread. I usually dig lumps out with a spoon.")

10. In a small skillet, heat enough olive oil to coat the bottom of the pan over medium heat. Fry each of the flatbreads until the bottoms are browned and toasted, adding more oil to the pan as needed. Then run them under the broiler until the fat is melting and the edges start to char, about 5 minutes.

11. Top the finished flatbreads with a nice sprinkling of capers, pickled onions and chiles, and plenty of parsley leaves. Eat immediately.

54. LOIS THE PIE QUEEN

@bambambaklava WHEN IN OAKLAND YOU MUST I MEAN MUSSSSSSST VISIT THE LEGENDARY LOIS THE PIE QUEEN AND ORDER THE REGGIE JACKSON SPECIAL AND A PECAN WAFFLE WITH FRIED CHICKEN SMOKED TURKEY GREENS & RICE AND BEANS!!!!!! TRUST. #fuckthatsdelicious

NOTE: The Reggie Jackson Special is two fried pork chops, two eggs, grits, hash browns or rice, plus biscuits and coffee or milk.

Chris Davis, son of Lois, father of our friend Garrett from the band Trash Talk.

55.

MOR

CcO

The best thing that happened in Morocco was because of what didn't happen. We were on our way up into the Atlas Mountains to meet with a Berber woman to bake bread with her, but we never made it because it was an impossible trek. Our guides kept saying, *Fifteen minutes, fifteen minutes,* and it ended up being three hours into the Atlas Mountains and we were nowhere close. At the end of the day, they had no fucking idea where they were going, and we were just driving in a Japanese camel—this Toyota Land Cruiser—on this little side-of-the-mountain road that was dry and crumbly and looked like it could give way at any time: I was freaked out, nauseous, I had to take a piss. So we get out at the tip of this cliff—looking down, it's gorgeous—and we see some kid riding sidesaddle on a donkey on the phone texting. That's when I just said, *Take me back.*

On the way up there, hours before, we had gone through a village, so we stopped there on the way back and ate in a restaurant where you had to walk up about seventy-five stairs to get to where you needed to get to, the lambs you're going to eat just wandering around everywhere. We ordered little fresh-ground lamb kebabs simply charred over the charcoal. No sauce, no salt, no pepper, no flavoring in the lamb—just plain, tasty, beautifully clean meat. But then they serve it with sides of coarse salt and ground cumin, which they serve with all the roasted and grilled meats over there. So you sprinkle a little bit of salt and cumin on every piece as you eat. It's fucking phenomenal, and I did the exact replica of that meal as soon as I got home on the Bukharian Jewish grill I tell you about on page 168.

56. NATURAL WINES

For a long time, I didn't drink that much of anything. I don't like liquor, I don't drink a lot of beer, and I didn't like wine at all. But when I went to Paris in 2015, I met the homey Clovis at this pizza shop. He was there bringing them natural wine, because he's a distributor. Clovis is actually from Macedonia, where my family moved after they left Albania, so we just hit it off. His real name is Goran, which is a Balkan name, but everybody calls him Clovis. Clovis changed my life, because he put me on to natural wines: I was drinking them the rest of that trip. They tasted so good—like juice—and they made me feel so good. Natural is like a drug—like just after you've taken mushrooms and you're laughing a lot. It's just fucking fun, like dancing to Latin music on a summer day.

Normally with the regular aging process of wine—which I know everyone cherishes—it just doesn't leave a good flavor in my mouth. It makes everything really dry and tart, and it often tastes like rubbing alcohol to me. But then with this natural wine, it was, *Wow, this is alive, this is giving me energy, this is just juice directly derived from the grape.* With natural wines, there's not been so much processing, nothing added, like regular wines. The best are just the grape and nature, relying on the unknown: The yeasts are from the fruit itself, the skins are left on, and the grapes are left to do their own thing. It's everything that I am about: It's artisan-made. It's special. It's all-naturale. It's done with love, done with care. Clovis likes to say natural wine is a way of thinking.

I like natural wines that are within a year or two of being made—within a year, even. I just don't like the development on older wines. I dig the idea—I feel it. But I like to drink them young: I like the young fruit. I like the bubbling from natural fermentation at that stage—I love things that are alive and vibrant-tasting and new and funky and weird and still taste like grapes. With spontaneously fermented beer—where they use natural yeasts too—it's almost the same thing. Over time, I've learned some words to describe the wines I like: Juicy. Nonstructured. Young. Cloudy. Skin-contact. If a wine person doesn't know what I am talking about after that, then they just don't know.

The wine that I really fell in love with thanks to Clovis is a rosé called Susucaru from this guy Frank Cornelissen in Sicily, in Mt. Etna. It's fucking tremendous, everything I just described above. I've mentioned it on TV a couple of times, and now I even have fucking hood dudes hitting me up for the natural wine: *Yo, that shit look good, son, where can I get me some of that, where can I get the Su-su-cah-ru.* I have talked about it so much that the dude who distributes Susucaru in the States told me he's getting random calls from liquor stores in the Bronx who want to carry it. I am like a wine celebrity, ha ha—I feel like I am swaying a lot of people who wouldn't usually be into natural wine, which I love. I am not the foremost expert on it, for sure, but I feel like I get it. I just want to put everybody on to it, because I love it.

"NO THANKS— I PREFER IT *ALL-NATURALE!*"

I like all the natural beverages, like the sake I had at the best restaurant in Asia, Les Créations de Narisawa in Tokyo. I was hanging with Chef Yoshihiro Narisawa in the kitchen and he gave me two bottles of the rarest natural sake, because the man who grows his rice also makes just ten bottles of sake a year. Chef gave me two of them—that's love.

Giving thanks to the gods after a feast of Colombian food at one of the highest points in Barcelona.

OCTOPUS

I almost feel bad eating octopus, because it's such a majestic thing, such a perfect, elegant animal. They can change colors, they create electricity, and, of course, the anatomy of an octopus is unreal. It's ancient like an alligator, one of these creatures that have always been on this earth. I feel like when you eat octopus, you almost gain some kind of power or knowledge, an inner understanding. I've only become acquainted with the octopus recently, because I didn't eat seafood growing up. For some reason, I was scared of it. But now that I have traveled and seen these things, and I am diving with them and swimming with them, I am obsessed with them. I think Michael Voltaggio started my whole love affair with octopus, because he made it for me at his restaurant in Los Angeles like a chicken souvlaki. He literally just freestyled a dish for me a few years ago, an octopus and cauliflower dish sprinkled with shawarma spice—garlic, coriander, fennel, star anise, and smoked paprika. He added raisins plumped in grape juice, fried cauliflower pieces, and a cauliflower puree almost like a hummus. It was stupid good.

Since then, I have been eating a lot of it, making a lot of it in all kinds of ways. My mind is always on octopus: I've smoked it at home with jerk spices I got in Jamaica, or I bake it and top it with herbs and blood orange juice. I get the fusilli with baby octopus and bone marrow at Michael White's place Marea, another one of my favorite pastas, and I get the octopus at Babbo every single time I go. I got it five ways at Bobo Pulpín in Barcelona (see page 101), where I learned not to peel the skin off your octopus because it has a lot of collagen and there's a lot of health in there for you. I made fried octopus tacos with cheese at Hija de Sánchez in Copenhagen, the taco stand opened by Rosio Sanchez, a former Noma chef. There I learned that deep-frying octopus is genius, because then when you cut into it, the outside is crispy and the inside is soft and perfect. Just like Mario taught me: You either cook octopus for two hours or two minutes, otherwise it's chewy.

E-Z OVEN OCTOPUS

And that's it, it's going to be perfect.

MAKES 1 OCTOPUS

This is how Mario taught me to cook an octopus. I was chilling at home one night and I had a hankering, so I texted him, *Yo, how do I make octopus?* And I learned how to make octopus in one text.

1 (2–3 pound, 1–2.5 kg) octopus, beak removed
Extra virgin olive oil
4 large cloves garlic, crushed
8 Calabrian chiles
1 wine cork

1. Preheat the oven to 330°F (160°C).

2. Put the octopus in a terra-cotta type of baking dish, like earthenware, then massage it with the olive oil. Throw in the garlic and chiles and the cork and cover the dish with aluminum foil. Bake it for 2 hours. You chill out. Smoke a bunch of joints, hit a bunch of dabs.

3. You can now take this any way you want: You could eat it with tapenade, or with some chopped-together herbs with a little bit of oil, salt, and lemon, kind of like free-form chimichurri. You could dip it in My Special Sauce from page 189. You could *agrodolce* it in something sweet and sour, like vinegar and honey. You can peel off the skin or leave it on. What I like to do is peel off some of the gooey skin and leave the suckers, then get a cast-iron pan burning hot and char it. Throw the baby on the plate, squeeze some lemon over, and finish it with some gorgeous olive oil and salt.

FROM VERSE 3, "IT CONCERNS ME" ON *BLUE CHIPS 2*:

"Greek men, jump off the back of
the boat for dinner
Barehanded snatch up an octopus
I'm a winner
Grill it, hit it with olive oil
and lemon
Then kiss my fingers, *efharisto*
that was delicious"

I like to paint pictures with my raps. My old Greek landlord used to tell me about how he would dive off the boat to get the octopus growing up in Greece. He's like a sixty-year-old guy. I could just imagine him mad old, jumping over the back of the boat grabbing the octopus with his hands. I don't know if he did all that, but I will say he committed a mass murder of squirrels in Queens. I was sitting there at three in the morning one time, and I hear some crazy screeching and scratching in the ceiling. *What the fuck is going on?* I was just sitting there watching sports ass-naked probably—smoking, eating cereal—and I hear some kind of battle royal up there, like a royal rumble of squirrel. This continued for weeks, but my Greek landlord didn't believe me—he thinks I am just high, this stoner imagining things. One night I am lying on the couch, and for some reason I look up on top of the kitchen cabinet, and I make eye contact with a fucking black ninja squirrel that broke through the wall of my apartment. We looked directly at each other and I screamed at him, like a pirate—*rarghh!*—and I threw the remote control from the TV at the cabinet. It was a scene. I woke up everybody in my building: I started hitting the cabinets, breaking them down—*boom-boom-boom!*—I made my landlord get up and hammer a piece of wood across the hole. But the squirrels were still relentless, and they ate a hole through that. He eventually captured them with peanut butter and traps and got rid of them. You want to know why that happened? Because I used to always have cereal in my house, that's why.

58. KOWLOON CHAR SIU BAO

Do you know how many people send me messages on Instagram and Twitter telling me they have been to Kowloon Restaurant & Cake Shop in London's Chinatown on my recommendation, telling me that their pork bun is the most incredible thing they have ever tasted? It's a soft, sweet yeast bun (the *bao*) filled with sticky, bright-red barbecued pork (the *char siu*). It's so good, it's ridiculous—and I've had pork buns all over the world. I grew up in Flushing, Queens, remember, the most densely Asian area there is in New York City, and I can tell you there is not one that compares to that one right there.

59. HOT DOGS

Hot dogs have been a major part of my life for as long as I can remember, and they're almost as important as a bagel or a hamburger. My mother would always have Hebrew National dogs in the fridge. (She gets on kicks and keeps weird things in the house, and then we get addicted to them, like Diet Cherry 7-Up. There would always be thirteen of them over by the radiator, waiting on the floor so we didn't have to go to the store all the time. Thirteen seltzers and thirteen Diet Cherry 7-Ups.) At home she would cook hot dogs in the pan, but at the Jewish deli, where they do them on a griddle, my mother would always get them well-done, which is where I first got the idea of crunch and well-doneness in a hot dog.

There's just something about going to the Jewish deli and getting one of those dogs that are straight burnt almost. Even at a barbecue, I love the last hot dog on the grill—it's given up all its fat and it becomes like a meringue cookie, porous and chalky. A Jewish deli hot dog has to have mustard on it. I used to do it with ketchup, which is like a wunderkondiment for me, but I grew up. Though I don't care how anyone eats their dog: I like mayo on it, I like mustard on it. I like it lots of ways. I even like hot dogs cut up and used as a flavoring agent for things like fried rice.

There are also *salchipapas*, or hot dogs and French fries fried together as they do in Latin America. How can it be bad to fry meat and a potato together in the same thing? The question is really where have they been my whole life, and where it's been has been Colombia. I've also had a Mission Street Mexican hot dog in San Francisco that was amazing. There was a man on the corner with a shopping cart and a sheet pan on top of the cart and a little fire going. I yell out to him from the car in Spanish, *Yo, what you have: Qué tienes*? He had hot dogs wrapped in bacon. So I jump out of the Jeep to get one of these beautiful mystery dogs and he's got some fucking onions frying on the sheet pan, and next to it are some serrano chiles that are blistered up and gorgeous. He also put ketchup, mustard, and mayo on it. I got in the car, gave everybody a little taste, and everyone was like, *Oh, shit*—they all wanted to go back.

But I'm telling you the Chicago dog is my favorite dog of all the hot dogs. I love sport peppers. I love that they put a pickle on it. I love the chopped onions, the relish, the poppy seed, a half a tomato. They griddle the shit out of them. I don't know the origin, I don't know why, I don't know what the fuck, but I know that shit is tremendous. It blows New York hot dogs out of the water for me.

EGG NOODLES WITH FETA AND PAPRIKA

Now this is a fucking pasta.

SERVES 1

I am just a pasta guy, a pasta addict. I've been eating pasta since I've been fucking born. The first pasta I ever had was the one my grandmother used to make all the time: Egg noodles with butter, paprika, a little red chile pepper if you want to get crazy, and feta cheese, always Bulgarian. Un-fucking-real. If you add a lot of black pepper, which my grandmother would never do, it makes this like an Albanian *cacio e pepe*.

4 ounces (100 g) wide egg noodles
¼ cup (½ stick) salted butter
4 ounces (114 g) Bulgarian sheep's milk feta cheese
1 teaspoon good-quality paprika

• •

1. Cook the egg noodles in a large pot of boiling, salted water until just al dente.

2. While the pasta cooks, melt the butter in a medium skillet over low heat.

3. When the pasta is ready, add it directly to the skillet with a few spoonfuls of the pasta cooking water.

4. Add the paprika and toss to coat, then add the feta and do the same, adding a little pasta water if needed to loosen up the sauce or cooking it for a few seconds to thicken it. Sprinkle on a little more feta over the top, if you have some, and eat immediately.

SPAGHETTI WITH GARLIC, BEAUTIFUL OLIVE OIL, AND CHILES

It's hot, but that's how I go.

SERVES 1

My famous pasta dish, the standard that I will make for the rest of my life, is spaghetti with soft garlic browned in extra virgin olive oil and burnt chiles—you just have to toast them to get the good flavor.

1 big handful spaghetti
½ cup extra virgin olive oil, plus more for drizzling
3 large cloves garlic, crushed, peeled, and sliced
1–2 teaspoons Calabrian chiles
Freshly ground black pepper

1. Cook the spaghetti in a large pot of boiling, salted water until just al dente.

2. While the pasta cooks, heat a skillet over medium heat and add ½ cup of the greenest olive oil you can find, then add the garlic and the chiles, adding the full amount if you like things hot. I chop them up first, which makes it even hotter.

3. Let the chiles and garlic cook just a minute or two, until the garlic is just barely brown. If the pasta is not ready yet, remove the pan from the heat so the garlic doesn't burn.

4. When the spaghetti is just al dente, add it and 2 to 3 large spoonfuls of the pasta cooking water to the skillet and return the heat to medium. Cook, tossing the pasta frequently, until the pasta is cooked through, the garlic is soft, and there isn't too much liquid left in the pan.

5. Drizzle it with lots more olive oil, grind mad amounts of black pepper over the top, and eat immediately—maybe even straight out of the pan.

EGG NOODLES
WITH FETA
AND PAPRIKA

SPAGHETTI WITH GARLIC, BEAUTIFUL OLIVE OIL, AND CHILES

62

CACIO E PEPE

In Rome, I had *cacio e pepe* every-place I went. It's always done with the *tonnarelli* pasta in Rome, always with black pepper and Pecorino Romano, but every place I went the Pecorino they used was a slightly different maker or different age, which is cool as a motherfucker. When it's too old, it's like, *Come on now*. I feel only hard-core cacio people can handle that. I love cacio e pepe, and then I get over there in Rome where the fucking dish was invented, and I wasn't prepared for that intensity. I learned how to make it, how you have to make a paste: Grind mad amounts of the cheese and black pepper, add a little olive oil, a little bit of hot pasta water from the pot where the pasta is cook-ing—then when the pasta is done you add it to the paste with a little more pasta cooking water and more black pepper, and that's the sauce. Me, I always reinforce the pepper—I want a heavy taste of that, I love it. And the pasta must be perfectly al dente: If you cook pasta into mush, I hate you. Sounds fucking easy, but holy shit, that is a difficult dish to make if you don't know what you're doing.

On that same trip to Rome, we went to Osteria de Fontanelle in Traste-vere, the neighborhood just over the river from central Rome. We made pasta with an amazing woman, who does it sitting in a chair at the window. She's about four feet tall, four feet wide: Amazing. She let me cut some fettuccine with her and I was fucking it up, so she was yelling at me. She definitely has one of those slick mouths on her, talking mad shit, like Poochie, who works at the Weiner Circle hot dog stand in Chicago, where we filmed *Fuck, That's Delicious*. (Poochie gives you a hard time, but you know she has all this love in her heart for you.) I first learned how to make fresh pasta from Mario years ago, watching him on TV. I make a well of flour, crack the egg into the well, whisk it with a fork until it becomes something, add a little cold water, then work it a little bit with an old wooden dowel from my grandmother that I just love. In Albania, the dowel and the *tepsia*, which is the circular metal dish that so many things are cooked in, are handed down for years. When any kitchen tool is really seasoned well, you can never get rid of it: It's like a smoker—you never fucking clean a smoker, because that seasoning makes you who you are as a cook.

LILIA'S AGNOLOTTI

63.

My current favorite pasta right now is at Lilia in Brooklyn. Chef Missy Robbins's agnolotti are some of the most incredible things you'll ever taste: They're made with feta, saffron, thyme, honey, and these oven-roasted tomatoes that aren't San Marzano but are from just down the way in Italy. It's sick shit. The stuffed pasta programs at Babbo and Marea, Chef Michael White's place,* are also incredible.

 I actually met Chef through music, because he was a fan. He just came up to me at the Miami Food & Wine Festival in 2013, showing me his phone—he had my album on it. He's the fucking man, and the very first show I did for Vice was a six-course meal with Body at his restaurant Marea in Manhattan. Since then, I've eaten at all his places many, many times, made pasta by hand and risotto and crudo with him, and seen all kinds of things in his kitchen. Whenever our show goes to these fancy places, Michelin-starred restaurants and ones on the world's fifty best list, there's no chance I'll ask to eat there. What I really want is a kitchen experience, watching a chef at work. That way it's not just me and my friends sitting around a table talking shit—which I do too—but a chance to stand next to someone while they are creating magic. It's like being in the room while Picasso is painting, or while Usher is making a song.

64.

BAKED ZITI

Baked ziti is underappreciated, but it's just fire. That browned cheese on top? It's the Maillard reaction—that's always what I am about. There's also the stuffed shell—that's nostalgia food, that's public-school food: One of my earliest introductions to pasta was getting stuffed shells for lunch at school.

ACTION BRONSON'S MYSTERIES OF ANCIENT ROME

AS TOLD TO RACHEL WHARTON AFTER A GREAT MANY DABS ONE RAINY MORNING IN JUNE

Great place. Ancient walls. Everything around was there before you, many, many, many thousands of years before you. It's like a social studies book. Just traveling around Rome you see that they had running water—hot and cold water—for thousands of years. Somehow they were getting everything right at that time, and then it just stopped. How did that happen? Everything was right, and then it just fell. Like the monuments that they were able to construct trump anything that man does today—this stonemason work, specifically coming from the Romans and the Tuscans. They showed the world how to work with stone and marble. It's beyond massive columns: The Pantheon to this day is the oldest freestanding dome structure ever constructed. There's no support to the dome in the Pantheon: It's a marvel of architecture—can't figure out how to do it. There are so many things Leonardo da Vinci designed, and those ancient works of art. Everything is precious. It seems every corner is gated, something is blocked off, and then you see these humongous obelisks carved with Egyptian hieroglyphs just standing in the middle of squares, like, *What the fuck is going on?* The carvings of these battles are the purest expression of art—they have some columns leading up to one of the castles, Castel Sant'Angelo in Rome, and there are some works on the columns that are dated to about a thousand years ago. And it's mediocre work, it's mediocre stone work. It's good—but compared to fucking ten thousand years ago, it's child's play. The intricacies of the work that was done back then: Mind-fucking-boggling. Changed my life. I don't know how the shit happened. But to just be near it—to eat raw scampi fifty steps away. Life is mind-blowing—you gotta respect people that came before us and where we are. I don't really know how to explain the type of respect you need, you just need this awareness. You just need this overall awareness of who we are, and that shit is crazy. Bottom line, shit's crazy.

65.

MAZZO'S PASTA WITH PEPPERONI CRUSCHI

This couple Francesca Barreca and Marco Baccanelli made me some of the best things that I had in all of Rome at their restaurant Mazzo. They are on the cutting edge of Roman cuisine—the traditionalists probably don't like them, but they don't give a shit, because they're young and full of new ideas and shit like that. They make this pasta with crunchy sweet red chiles that have been dried and fried. No spice— just deep, smoky sweetness. It's crazy, just olive oil and those chiles. They make another with that and mackerel.* I hate mackerel, but they made me like mackerel.

*

66

DON PEPPE'S LINGUINE CLAMS

Don Peppe is this amazing old family-style Italian place in Ozone Park, Queens, between the Aqueduct Race-track and JFK Airport, with the jockeys' jerseys on the walls and no menu except for what's written on the wall. You always have to get the linguine with clams, with dozens of garlic cloves fried in olive oil until golden brown, soft, and sweet, and chopped Long Island littlenecks. Once you've had those clams, it's hard to have any others.

CAST OF CHARACTERS

ACTION

MEYHEM

BODY

RACHEL

NO PICTURE AVAILABLE
WAITERS

THE FOLLOWING DISCUSSION TOOK PLACE OVER LUNCH AT DON PEPPE'S, APRIL 12, 2016:

ACTION: This place you never leave fucking hungry, never. I've never left here hungry; I've always left here waddling.

MEYHEM: You've never left without a shopping bag.

ACTION: Walking and waddling.

MEYHEM: I did a half hour on the treadmill before I came here, because I knew what I was going to do when I got here.

AcTION: So now you're all good.

BODY: Even it out.

BODY: We have to hit haze, we have so many things to talk about—rap things, slash things we have to discuss. We have to hit haze.

ACTION: Is haze man open right now? (to Rachel) You're going to come with us to buy weed.

RACHEL: OK.

BODY: And listen to eighties rock on the way there and get emotional. You're going to forget you saw tears in my eyes.

ACTION: What do you think we listened to on the way here? "Hold the line."

BODY: (eating clams) It's so good, it's kind of crazy. (to waiter) Yes, we need the lemon please.

ACTION: (to Meyhem) You killed that Jamaican song. June plum. I started laughing: "Juice dripping down my chest."

MEYHEM: Drinking out of the goblet.

ACTION: The visual is next level.

ACTION: (holding up photo of octopus he cooked on *Late Night with Seth Meyers*) Did you see the picture of these? A humongous octopus. It actually wasn't that big. Three and a half pounds. Yo, the food stylist, she might have made it too soft. I have never had it that soft. I feel like I told her exactly how I wanted it, and she refused to do what I wanted to do. I told her not to add celery and not to add parsley, and she put both of those things. It's disrespectful—just chiles, cork, and garlic—no liquid. I got

that recipe directly from Batali. I said Batali, yo, I got this octopus, how do I do it. He said, OK, 330 in the oven, for two hours, Calabrian chiles, olive oil, and whole cloves of garlic. I still have the text. I always do it at 350—he probably has the Viking oven. Son, Kevin Costner was there. He said *what's up* when we first came in. He was there at the Seth Meyers show.

BODY: Yo, *Dances with Wolves*.

ACTION: That's what I said. Everybody else was like, some other movie.

BODY: *The Postman*.

ACTION: *Tin Cup*.

RACHEL: Is that a real movie?

BODY: It's like a golf movie, he's like a scumbag golf guy.

ACTION: You have to be really bored at the crib when you see it.

ACTION: There was also that chick from the zombie movie. It's on UPN? No, PIX channel 11.

RACHEL: She eats brains and solves crimes because she can see what happened in their recent history.

BODY: So it's like a Sunday afternoon type of thing.

RACHEL: No, Sunday afternoons are Patrick Swayze movies.

BODY: Oh damn, you know the best one?

RACHEL: *Road House.*

BODY: *Ghost.*

RACHEL: *Ghost?*

BODY: I want to get that Puerto Rican guy and put him on the show and praise him. Like, you're a legend, you made that movie.

ACTION: Remember in the train station, and he's like biting him?

RACHEL: My god I do not remember any of that.

BODY: Shit, Patrick Swayze.

RACHEL: There was a big picture of him when I went to NBC last night, from his appearances on *Saturday Night Live.* On the wall in guest services. Did you have to go through there?

ACTION: Amazing. It would be good to be enshrined like that. Just a picture of us up on the wall, you know, as commemoration.

BODY: Like a plate.

ACTION: We should get an ill plate made of us. A commemorative plate. A bunch of jerks already did that.

BODY: But have Alchemist's face crossed off.

MEYHEM: Put some sauce right where his face is.

ACTION: Yeah, he's not on it.

BODY: We should put his face on ashtrays.

ACTION: (looking at another table being served dessert) What the fuck is that?

BODY: It's cake, some sort of cake.

RACHEL: I think you guys should have a plate.

ACTION: Something like that—a plate or a spoon.

MEYHEM: Body's face is built for a spoon.

ACTION: You know what's funny? You know who does that engraving? That dude Bert. Bert does that shit. When you give him a spoon, and you can put your face right on the spoon with one of those etching things.

BODY: Perfect, we'll do it.

ACTION: I've seen him put a big spiderweb on a spoon with one of those engraving things. I think I am going to get a skull put on my knife.

BODY: With ruby eyes.

BODY: (to Rachel) Is this your first time here?

RACHEL: Did one of you find it first?

ACTION: (pointing to Body) Well, he lives in the neighborhood. I feel like you've always known about it. Have you always known about it?

BODY: Nah, I remember my mom took me here one time back in the day, but I heard about it when that show was going on, *Entourage.*

RACHEL: They came here?

BODY: Yeah, they talked about it a lot.

MEYHEM: I knew about this for a long time.

BODY: It's one of those places that don't advertise—they don't deliver, they don't advertise, you just know about it on Lefferts over here.

ACTION: It's dead, it's like Death Valley. It's in between JFK and where it's residential.

RACHEL: How long has it been here?

ACTION: (to Meyhem) How long have you been coming here?

MEYHEM: Since I was about fifteen, sixteen.

RACHEL: Would you come here by yourself or would your parents bring you?

MEYHEM: I brought myself.

ACTION: You came here at sixteen years old by yourself?

MEYHEM: You know what, I used to go to Adam's Night School, that's when I found out about it, it spoke to me.

RACHEL: Would they put you in the middle of a table?

MEYHEM: They put me in the corner.

BODY: He was near the bathroom, after he fixed the toilet. Thanks, Gus.

MEYHEM: Me, my family, my parents knew about it too.

ACTION: (to waiter) Yo, how long you guys been here?

WAITER: (with heavy Italian accent) In this location 1968, we move from Brooklyn in 1968.

ACTION: And before?

WAITER: Cleveland and Liberty, thirty, forty years.

ACTION: East New York used to be predominantly Italian. Now it's not—now it's all Puerto Rican and Dominican.

RACHEL: That's the home of *Goodfellas.*

ACTION: *Goodfellas.* John Gotti's thing is right here on 101, right?

BODY: Yeah, 101 his club, his social club, the fish and hunting club. The place is still there. I don't know if the club is still there, the building is. I don't know about the actual hunting club.

BODY: We knew this Italian kid we used to hang out with sometimes, he had a rotten mouth, like he refused to brush his teeth. He was on strike.

RACHEL: Does he have any teeth?

ACTION: His teeth were hanging on for dear life.

MEYHEM: They looked like little shards.

RACHEL: Like niblets.

BODY: He was caught up in the struggle, man.

MEYHEM: Imagine when he hears he made the book and then he's like, *Yo I made the book*, and then he's like, *that's how I got in?*

BODY: Those tar pits.

BODY: I haven't had any sleep but I'm just thrilled to be here right now.

MEYHEM: I'm very well rested.

ACTION: (to Body) You didn't sleep at all.

BODY: Like an hour, on the plane.

BODY: This is what I sent pictures of to everybody this morning early—this is hip-hop right here, gold chain, rap, backwards cap, against the rules.

—one minute of silence passes—

MEYHEM: Make sure to mention when we have a meal we all stare at our phones and don't talk.

BODY: Right now I am actually cursing Matt Raz.

RACHEL: Are you actually talking to each other?

ACTION: I'm looking at Twitter. I gotta do quality control. I gotta make sure that the song has been posted everywhere. If it don't get posted to certain sites, I'm going to be pissed.

RACHEL: Who's supposed to do that?

ACTION: Bunch of people—there's no one really that I can point my finger at and say, *You fucked up.*

RACHEL: Can you do it?

ACTION: Yeah, but I shouldn't have to. I pay other people to do it—I have to do it, then I'm gonna be upset.

WAITER: Linguine white clams.

BODY: It's like soup in there.

ACTION: You've never had the lingine and white clams? What the fuck are you saying to me now? This is like the national dish here.

ACTION: This is next level, don't even wait.

RACHEL: I kinda wanted to stare at it for a little while.

ACTION: Chef Michael is a special guy. Man, he was about to take it away from you and give it to me.

RACHEL: Twenty-five bucks.

BODY: Never best for less.

BODY: You love that, don't you.

BODY: It's an emotional dish.

RACHEL: There must be like thousands of garlic cloves back there.

ACTION: Yo, it's out of control. Try it without chile, try it straight up—and then hit it with the spice if you want.

RACHEL: Cleveland and Liberty, that's what they said?

ACTION: Yep.

BODY: Danza's from out there too. Tony Danza. The young Danza.

ACTION: The texture, it's perfect, right. It's like chewy, and just al dente.

BODY: Just before it's done.

ACTION: He has it down pat. Think it takes like eight minutes to get it like this.

BODY: I don't like pasta when it's hard— try to do it al dente and you don't know what you're doing. It's like, c'mon.

BODY: That's how you mess up the Chef Boyardee. You gotta defrost first.

MEYHEM: You have to defrost it.

ACTION: (to Body) Yo, I got a rough cut of Hawaii, when you say you perform like circus de olé . . . oh my god, circus de olé.

BODY: Then when you told me what it really was? All my life I thought it was circus de olé.

ACTION: You were like, *When I perform it's like circus de olé.*

RACHEL: That's fucking awesome, though.

ACTION: Do you know how intense Cirque du Soleil is? That's what I was like, circus de olé. I love it.

BODY: That's how my performance is.

BODY: Imagine we tell Chris he's replaced with Matt Raz.

ACTION: Hey, listen, Matt Raz has been on the team since the beginning.

BODY: Remember when we did the podcast, and he came in his own cab just to be there. He was like, *I don't need to do nothing, I just want to be here for the moment.* We should do an episode here, just sayin'.

MEYHEM: They might not want that here.

BODY: I feel like they don't want that here, but they might let you do it. You.

ACTION: That's the thing.

BODY: In a certain way.

ACTION: I'm good enough just coming here. Just coming here.

BODY: I mean it was on *Entourage.*

RACHEL: Did they actually come in here?

ACTION: No, but they have a T-shirt and they talk about it.

BODY: It was like two or three episodes too, somebody must have come here and really loved it.

ACTION: That's the funny part, that they were all supposed to be from Queens.

BODY: We got chicken on the way, it's good to start off with seafood, build it up.

MEYHEM: I slept till noon, I woke up a new song was out, it's making noise, so now I'm like here having breakfast in the middle of the day.

BODY: You know about eating soup before you start a meal or anything?

MEYHEM: No, I don't.

BODY: It opens up the palate and all that.

ACTION: I didn't know that, I thought that soup came after.

BODY: Old Italian man told me that. Always start with soup—open you up and get you ready.

MEYHEM: For your organs, make space.

BODY: The palate.

ACTION: Sometimes you know when I was back at my grandma's house she would just make me straight-up soup with cabbage salad. I love it. Cabbage salad with like apple cider vinegar and that was it. Cabbage was sort of this weird funky sweet tasting with some vinegar on it. It's like, *Whoa, what's this*?

BODY: Like a fire coleslaw. Cabbage is slept on, but you can spice it and do so many things with it.

ACTION: I love it.

BODY: It absorbs it, you know.

ACTION: You know stewed cabbage is like one of the craziest things ever.

MEYHEM: My mother makes this curry cabbage.

ACTION: (looking at a guy walking through the dining room) Check out this dude.

BODY: It's like, *Yeah my dick is on the floor, they don't even make trousers that big.*

ACTION: You gotta walk like you got the golden wang, right?

BODY: A pair of pliers holding it up.

MEYHEM: Don't fill up on pasta, I have chicken to annihilate.

RACHEL: Fifty bucks worth of chicken.

MEYHEM: I ate every piece of clam out of it, though, I am trying, man. Getting on treadmills and trying to eat a little bit less starch, doing what I can till I have to do what I have to do.

RACHEL: Till more carbs. I love carbs, all of them.

ACTION: I ate a bagel with cheese this morning, and then I ate a straight bagel without anything on it. We went to Uto-pia this morning, me and my mom after I drove my kids to school. Real early.

MEYHEM: Did I tell you about the new cream cheese they have at Baker's Dozen? Birthday cream cheese.

ACTION: That sounds terrible.

MEYHEM: It's ridiculous.

ACTION: Why is everything tie-dyed and rainbow-flavored right now? Tie-dye bagel, rainbow bagel?

MEYHEM: Yeah, that's crazy, who wants food coloring on their bagel.

ACTION: I fucking hate it.

BODY: It's like the red velvet shit that happened a few years ago—everything was red velvet.

ACTION: Everything was red velvet now everything is fucking tie-dyed.

RACHEL: Or cronut-ed.

MEYHEM: Those are good.

ACTION: I've never had one, but I'm saying how much better could they be than a regular fucking doughnut? I mean c'mon.

MEYHEM: The texture might be.

ACTION: I like croissant, but I don't like croissant that much. One thing I don't like about a croissant is holding the shit and it crumbles all over your face and being all buttery in your hand. My favorite doughnut at this point in life is the crème brûlée doughnut from Doughnut Plant.

BODY: Yeah, that's a fire one.

ACTION: So they make this little doughnut hole type of thing, and fill it with crème anglaise and put that hard top on it, it's unbelievable. You should please try that one. You get that crunch and the creaminess.

ANOTHER WAITER: (with strong Italian-American accent) Another bottle of water over deh, guys?

ACTION: Please.

ANOTHER WAITER: I saw you were dry.

MEYHEM: Like any doughnut with maple. Good old-fashioned maple doughnut.

RACHEL: I like an old-fashioned jelly doughnut. If they're good, they put real jelly.

BODY: I don't like this little skimp. They got to put jelly. Diner style if they're jelly they got to put jelly, and the powder like *bombolinis*.

ACTION: Now we're talking.

ANOTHER WAITER: Love the doughnuts.

ACTION: The bombolinis that they make where they fry them and dip them in honey? Which ones are those? And then you put the sprinkles on them? Which ones are those?

RACHEL: And then you build a tower?

ACTION: Yeah, what's that?

ACTION: I've seen Batali make those so many times. The Italian holiday doughnut.

RACHEL: Are you looking it up?

ACTION: Yeah, the *fritelli*.

RACHEL: (pointing to phone) OK. So that's a bombolini filled with jelly down there.

ACTION: Remember when we had them at Marea? And they brought cream and all sorts of different things.

ANOTHER WAITER: You guys want to keep the bread or no?

BODY: Talking about soup right dude, the dude from Mitchell & Ness just hit me up. Blowing my mind, *Yo what's good*?

ACTION: I wanted to go today to Philly.

BODY: It's not even that far—two-and-a-half-hour drive.

RACHEL: See those are just bombolini, filled. Speaking of doughnuts and Philly, have you been to Federal Donuts in Philly? If you go, you have to go there.

MEYHEM: I have heard of them.

RACHEL: Don't they make a maple doughnut for the fried chicken?

ACTION: They make a maple fried chicken doughnut?

RACHEL: They only serve it with the fried chicken. A maple doughnut, and it's the best doughnut.

BODY: Is it the one with the bacon on it?

RACHEL: When you order fried chicken, they put a maple doughnut in there.

ACTION: It sounds amazing.

MEYHEM: We have to go to Philly to get tattoos, doughnuts, chicken, jerseys, sneakers.

MEYHEM: You know when there's something on the menu called shrimp Luciano you gotta order it.

ACTION: You gotta order it, that's why we got the chicken Chinese—we never had that before.

RACHEL: It doesn't sound very Chinese.

ACTION: Sausage.

RACHEL: I guess they stuff chickens with sausage. Though I guess it's ducks.

ACTION: I don't think that's what it is, I feel like it's cacciatore with sausage in it.

ACTION: (to first waiter) Why the fuck is it Chinese chicken, tell me why?

WAITER: Because when Chinese people come, they want that one. People order it and they say, *I thought it was Chinese food*, and I say, *No, it's cacciatore*.

ACTION: That's awesome.

RACHEL: Oh, I forgot about the broccoli, it's like broccoli steaks.

MEYHEM: Give me a little plate.

ACTION: This *francese* is banging. You know what the absolute best flavor in the world is? Haze mixed with hard-core.

BODY: Wax?

ACTION: No, weed, son. When I tell you it tastes like cleaning product?

BODY: I love the wax with the haze.

ACTION: It tastes like cleaning product, like Pledge. So full.

BODY: That's such a crazy dish right there, it's regal.

ACTION: That's good, but that's better.

RACHEL: It's like pizza sauce.

ACTION: With sausage.

MEYHEM: But that has a better name.

BODY: I am violently full, I need to smoke weed, blast in my face, throw things out of the window, I need to throw things off the FDR. Go buy Frostys and not finish them.

ACTION: I used to have to child-lock the windows so he wouldn't be able to throw things out of them.

BODY: It's a known fact my aim is so ridiculous, it's very crazy.

MEYHEM: I was driving home from a strip club and they were throwing soul food out the window—macaroni and cheese flying on the boulevard all over the car.

BODY: Dave kept screaming how he was going to kill everybody, then he took a whole plate of macaroni and cheese and just rocked some dude at the bus stop. I was like, *that's not how you end a night*.

ACTION: That's how you start it.

MEYHEM: It was five A.M., he was headed to work.

BODY: He had no business doing that, he had no reason to be standing around like that.

ACTION: And then he got hit with macaroni and cheese. ●

CHARRED BROCCOLI

SERVES 2

This dish evolved over time, beginning with the broccoli my mother used to put in a pasta salad. They make a similar thing at Don Peppe's (see page 160), but they let the broccoli steam and get soft, where I prefer it to still have some crunch.

1 small to medium head broccoli with stem intact
Extra virgin olive oil
Flaky sea salt

1. Cut the broccoli in half lengthwise, from the top of the florets to the end of the stem. (You sometimes see broccoli heads where the stem has been trimmed. I don't like the short stem ones. I like the stalk.)

2. Place the broccoli steaks on a plate and drizzle oil over them

generously—let it soak into them for about 10 minutes.

3. Heat a skillet large enough to fit both sides of the broccoli over medium-high heat until it is smoking hot.

4. Add just enough olive oil to coat the bottom of the pan with a thin layer.

5. Add the broccoli and press it into the pan cut-side down, and let it char and smoke in the hot skillet until the stem is black-brown.

6. Serve it charred-side up and sprinkled with sea salt.

CRUST/ CRUNCH

All the really good things in life have the brownness, the serious fucking crunch of the Maillard reaction, which is a chemical thing that happens when amino acids and sugars meet at a certain heat. I am all about the Maillard reaction, but I don't go for a fancy name like that. I prefer the words that describe the result of that reaction: the crisp, the developed and dark, the blackened, charred, and barbecued.

It was a late night in Copenhagen, and we were on a kebab run. Kebabistan serves meat from the spit, but we needed to taste the kebab made over the fire: the adana kebab, the chicken kebab, the ones shaped over the sharp metal skewers. We made our way across town from Kebabistan to Kösk Kebab, and it was packed out. So I just ordered the food and put the wooden number they gave us on top of the luxury vehicle we were in, which had tables and curtains and a tufted couch. I had them deliver the food—which was incredible—right out to the van in front of the restaurant.

★ 69. KEBABISTAN

Everyone in Copenhagen knowns Kebabistan: Say that shit and everyone's eyes light up. I first found out about it from Tommy Mas, my producer on the album *Dr. Lecter.* He is a great guy, and a food guy—he owns a falafel joint and a pita bakery in Brooklyn. He said, *You gotta go here.* So I went, I fell in love, and I have now eaten from Kebabistan a hundred times. To tell you the truth, after Meyhem, Body, and I ate at Noma, we went to Kebabistan. The guys at the counter there are from Yemen, Afghanistan, and Turkey, which is the home of the *döner kebab,* the Turkish version of shawarma. In Europe, everyone knowns the döner, where in New York you always see shawarma or gyro. They also make burgers and falafel, but everybody gets the shawarma—chicken or lamb or mixed. At Kebabistan, the lamb shawarma is a spit of layered meat instead of the log. I like log, but it's all filler garbage in there—bread and different types of weird meats. You really want the prime cuts, meaning the outer crispy edge that's been roasting for a minute. You can get that sliced onto pita, but I always get it on the fucking Turkish *bröd,* because on that crusty loaf of Turkish bröd the experience is next level. It is perfect for the shawarma, because the end result is just so much more satisfying. Each bite is so balanced. There's nothing on that sandwich that's useless: The bread, the meat, a warm red pepper spread, pale green pickled peppers, lettuce, tomato, white sauce, cabbage. There are three Kebabistans in Copenhagen, but I go to the one on Istedgade on what I call the heroin block, because you always see people nodding off all around the street. It's just three blocks from the flaeskesteg on page 89.

70. KING DAVID BAKERY

One of my favorite places in the world is a little Bukharian bakery in Kew Gardens Hills called King David Bakery.* *Bukharian* means Jews originally from Central Asia—now home to all the -stans—and King David is the name of a lot of Bukharian places. (You pronounce it *bu-harian*.) Most of them left after the end of the Soviet Union, and there are a lot of people from that part of the world in that part of Queens. Bukharian breads are baked pressed up against the wall of these big tandoori-like ovens. Most are flattish rounds of white bread with a pattern pressed in the middle with a wood stamp. The owner also makes a flatbread with rye seed in it and these little pockets with pumpkin, caraway seeds, and onions inside and sesame seeds on top. Oh-my-fucking-lord there's nothing like them. Me and my mother can tear down three each plus half a bread. The owner has another bakery a storefront down where the sign says PRESTIGE MEN'S BOUTIQUE, but he put some pizza ovens in there and is now just making more crazy shit.

I just found out about this bakery a few years ago. My mother and I used to buy the bread from this Bukharian store called Jasmine not that far away—we'd buy our feta cheese there, the dried chickpeas, and tea, and this amazing bread. And I also bought an old Bukharian grill, just a primal open thing, made for kebabs. But Jasmine sold the bread in individual plastic bags so it would steam and get soft as it cooled. We used to try to show up right on time to get them warm, so we could take it out of the plastic and store it in a brown paper bag before it was ruined. Then we started asking him where he got it, but the guy wouldn't tell me—he'd say, *Oh, we get it from over there* and just wave his hand, because he obviously wanted me to get it from him. So I would wait outside, hoping I would see where the bread truck came from. Eventually I found out that it was fucking down the block at King David. If you go to the bakery, he takes it directly from the oven and puts it into the brown bag and that's it—directly into mouth.

✳ Unfortunately, literally one week after we took these pictures, King David and their whole block burned down. It's such a tragedy.

A NEW YORK SLICE

In New York, tell me where you can't get a decent slice. Any neighborhood, anywhere, you can pretty much get a decent slice. But let me take you to the back blocks, where the locals walk, for my six favorite slices.

NEW PARK PIZZA:
HOWARD BEACH, QUEENS

This slice is incredible. They know pizza is a very delicate creature, the dough is a living thing, and you have to treat it as you would treat a child. The ovens have probably been there since it opened in 1956—so those ovens are seasoned for years and years and years. You place that living organism into that hot oven with all that seasoning, and it just gives it that incomparable burnt bottom, the best you can get on a New York slice. It has freckles of texture on the bottom. Usually you get a slice of the regular—the round pie, not the square, though it's good too. You get it toasted. One rule: Even if it's a fresh pie, I want you to put that slice back in the oven and toast it. If it's not crunchy on the bottom, I get angry. I found out about this place because Body lives nearby. Howard Beach is all Italians—this was all heavy-duty wise guys back in the day, everyone was connected.

#2

ALFIE'S PIZZA:
RICHMOND HILL, QUEENS

This is the best square slice in Queens: You bite in, it's like a pillow. There's a lightness to the crust like a French pastry chef made it. My boy Warren put me on to Alfie's—this and Golden Fountain (see page 199). He would always tell me Alfie's had the best square in the world, but I didn't believe him until I tried it. They're from Catania, and they've been making that slice since 1974.

#3

DANI'S HOUSE OF PIZZA:
KEW GARDENS, QUEENS

At Dani's it's the sweet sauce that gives it that incredible flavor—that's what it says on the T-shirts, "IT'S THE SWEET SAUCE"—and also the burnt pockets of beautiful cheese and that dope crust they make. Plus the owner's Albanian. It's just a great, big, thin slice—made since 1959. Sometimes I just need that sweet flavor of their sauce. It's like being a fucking cokehead.

173

4

LUCIA PIZZA:
FLUSHING, QUEENS

When I was kicked out of Bayside High School, I had to take the bus to Flushing to the school for fuckups instead. The bus stops right in front of Lucia's, which has been there since 1962. It's just up the hill from Main Street, across the street from Macy's, and you could order from a little window right on the sidewalk. The bus would leave me off right there, so how could I not? It's just a corner slice—but it's the perfect corner slice: Salty, greasy, and the cheese and sauce all melt together to become one.

#5

NAPOLI PIZZERIA & RESTAURANT:
FLUSHING MEADOWS, QUEENS

Here it's all about the baked ziti slice. It's two things in one that I love—baked ziti and pizza—and it blew my mind the first time I had it, which was when I was twelve or thirteen years old. It was like when I saw *Terminator 2* for the first time—that's what that slice means to me. It's sauce mixed with pasta, a good ricotta, and a crust crisp enough to support it all—all those details are important. I passed this love down to my child, and my daughter also likes that slice. Napoli is just across from my mother's house, and now it's owned by an Afghani dude, though my uncle once had the chance to take it over. We probably should have, because a pizzeria might be the longest-lasting food establishment in New York: Pizzerias never crash. If you find a storefront with an unused pizza oven, it's like finding gold.

#6

L&B SPUMONI GARDENS:
BENSONHURST, BROOKLYN

Growing up we stayed local for pizzerias—we didn't start to explore till later. My cousins from Brooklyn introduced me to L&B, which is an icon for their Sicilian square pizzas in huge sheet pans. Here, the corner slice is the key to life: This slice has more crust, and I love the crust—especially when they add a little bit of cheese and let it ride the crust up a little bit, which they do. At L&B you also must double-park, and you must get the spumoni. It's called Gardens because it's like a beer garden in front.

EATING PIZZA IN NAPLES

On my last trip to Italy, we drove down the coast to Naples to 50 Kalò di Ciro Salvo, recommended to us as the best pizzeria in the world. Naples-style pizza is with buffalo mozzarella, with San Marzano tomatoes, and it is cooked in a very hot wood-burning oven. It's puffy, thin, floppy. They told me it is not a Naples pizza if it doesn't flop. As a result you have to fold the end onto itself, and then bite into it: You flip up the droop and fold it over. Also, when it comes out of the oven it must sit for at least two minutes to congeal. So you have a glass of wine, whatever, however long it takes to set up. Otherwise, you cut it right away and it'll be all over the place. We also had *suppli al pomodoro,* or rice balls filled with mozzarella cheese and all kinds of unbelievable stuff. Also a special *cacio e pepe* type of fried *bucatini* balls: Like you would take a fork and spin up a strand of bucatini, fry it, and then remove the fork so you have that little circular bucatini pile with béchamel and lots of pepper. This is definitely not the only place to eat pizza in Naples, but it was banging. Though I'll admit, I had pizza late one night in the hotel in Rome that was as good. You know me, I am not the type of guy to only eat at a certain place: I need variety. I need a shitty slice sometimes, it's still good. I can get a great slice from Dani's House of Pizza, but I can also eat a fucking dollar slice from 2 Bros. in Manhattan and they can be equally satisfying, you know?

175

72. RUBI'S AT NEW MAXWELL STREET MARKET

This is a stall at Maxwell Street Market, an outdoor, year-round Sunday flea market in Chicago, and goodness gracious, it is amazing. The owner, he has the best market cry, this call he makes to draw attention to his stand. It's one of my favorite noises ever— it's his equivalent to the Jadakiss laugh or Jay Z and his *uh-huh*. It's what they do when they enter the song, to let you know who they are. I had every single taco Rubi's made and they were all phenomenal—*al pastor*, the fucking *mole poblano*, *huitlacoche*, *carne asada*, *nopales*, *hongos*, plus fire-grilled *cebollas* and some habanero-pickled onions, with a charred flavor on their tortillas because they had a lady making them and fire-roasting them right there. Just the smell of the smoke from the grill was intoxicating— even Alchemist loved it, and he doesn't eat anything. Meanwhile, they're playing the music of the old *rancheras*: Eating tacos outside in the street while listening to Vicente Fernandez sing "El Rey," there's something about that that just does it to me.

73. MANDEL CROISSANT

Democratic Coffee Bar was a few blocks from my hotel in Copenhagen the last time I stayed for the Roskilde Festival. It's in the Copenhagen main library. David Berson, the owner of Peter Luger Steak House in Brooklyn, was in town also, and he told me their *mandel croissant*, or almond croissant, was the best pastry he had ever tasted. I say it is the best pastry *I* have ever tasted. Democratic makes the best croissants—you can tell because they only bake a couple of things, and croissants of all types are most of them. Almonds are one of my favorite things, and the custard inside the mandel croissant—it's ridiculous, it's absolutely ridiculous. Oliver Oxfeldt, the owner of Democratic, says it's just eggs, almond paste, lots of butter, and lots of sugar. (While I was there, a famous barista from Hong Kong was also in there getting schooled.) This place looks like it could be in Brooklyn, right down to the *Yentl* record on the wall.

177

This is all Chicago: Below, Me and Meyhem working on our swing before our show at the North Coast Music Festival. Above, me with the good folks from Roister.

178

Fake Guy Fieri

74.

TWO-MINUTE TOMATO SAUCE

Get a can of San Marzano crushed tomatoes. Fry up three cloves of garlic, sliced, in a pan with a bunch of tablespoons of hot olive oil: Fry 'em up real nice. Put a couple of Calabrian chiles in that oil and fry those up. Throw a handful of fresh basil leaves into the oil, let them wilt, then dump in the San Marzanos. Stir for two minutes over medium heat, then let it sit. Add your salt, add your pepper, and it's ready to go. It's the best tomato sauce I ever had, and you don't have to cook it for hours.

SALSA MACHA AL ESTILO DE CARLOS

75

Carlos was a Mexican guy from Veracruz who worked as a dishwasher in the kitchen of my father's restaurant. The whole story of Carlos is ill: He was tall and slim and was always dancing around, shaking his little hips, and he could cook, he could fix the air conditioner or the stove, he was an ironworker, he created art, he would ride his bike to and fro every day miles to work, and he would always be the first one there in the morning and the one to stay late to clean. He has a wife and kids back home in Veracruz—he sends home money, like many Mexicans who work in kitchens do—but he would always end up meeting some barbaric-looking Thai woman on Roosevelt Avenue at the Laundromat or some such, looking for love. Carlos's wife made this famous sauce that she sent him from home—*salsa macha*, essentially a handful of whole *chiles de árbol* burnt in oil then mashed into a paste. In Spanish, *macha* is the feminine version of macho, or "tough," so the name is like a play on words, because this sauce was hot like asbestos. Carlos made it too: He and the other Mexicans in my dad's restaurant would be in the kitchen burning the chiles—I was like, *What the fuck are you doing?* Then I tasted it—such a deep, rich flavor, it is really remarkable how that enhances the flavors of the chiles. I now use that toasting method all the time when I am cooking chiles, to add to pasta or tomato sauces or so many things. Carlos also showed me how to use the salsa macha to make sick *costillas*, which is Spanish for pork ribs, by just boiling them for mad long. Eventually, once the water evaporates and they're frying in their own fat, you throw in some macha and let it brown for a few minutes, and then it's done. Easy. Amazing.

At my father's restaurant, I worked with Carlos and also my friend Jusaid from Puebla for ten years, and they both taught me a lot. How to make the most incredible *caldo de pollo*, or chicken soup Mexican-style with red chile and a little lime, and also how to pickle stuff, how to make rice. Every time I peeled a pineapple, my man Carlos would take the skin and squeeze it to make pineapple water, and he also taught me how to love grapefruit: He would poke holes in it, top it with honey, and put it in the microwave until it got juicy, which is the only way I'll eat it to this day. During off time, Jusaid would make lunch and teach me how to make a flan or green mole made with vegetables and cilantro, which is un-fucking-believable. And when we had to run errands really early in the morning, I would pick him up and he would take me to the tamale lady at Roosevelt Avenue and Junction Boulevard, and we'd get mad fucking tamales. Jusaid still works there in the same kitchen, in the restaurant that's there now. He and all the other Mexicans taught me Spanish, and in exchange I taught them a little English. They loved talking crazy and loved acting crazy, and they would only teach me how to say things like *puto*. That's what you learn in a kitchen—never how to have a nice conversation with your grandmother.

NUEVAS COSTILLAS EN SALSA MACHA

Rest assured, this is a fucking hot rib.

SERVES 2

The original salsa macha,* the one Carlos first taught me, is basically a whole bag of chiles de árbol toasted in vegetable oil until they start to smoke. I should say that I don't toast, I burn: The darker the color of the chiles, the more intense the flavor. Then you just grind it all down—I sometimes also add sesame seeds. I like this version better for the ribs, because the peanuts and chipotles add nuttiness and smokiness, and the sugar and the vinegar caramelize when you fry them in the pork fat. It's also not as hot.

1 to 1½ pounds (455 to 680 g) pork spareribs or baby backs

1 cup (240 ml) not very fancy extra virgin olive oil

3 cloves garlic, crushed with the side of a knife and peeled

4 medium chipotle (or morita) chiles, stems removed

10 dried chiles de árbol, stems removed

3 tablespoons raw shelled peanuts

1 tablespoon sesame seeds

Salt

2 tablespoons dark brown sugar

1 tablespoon white vinegar

---

* The OG Salsa Macha: Fry 3 crushed garlics and ¼ big white onion in ½ cup (120 ml) olive oil in a skillet until brown. Add 20 chiles de árbol, toast until dark brown, and add ½ tablespoon sesame seeds. When the seeds are golden brown, remove the skillet from the heat, add a pinch of salt, let cool, and then puree.

1. Cut the ribs roughly into 4-inch- (10-cm-) wide pieces—they don't have to be an exact size; this is just so they fit in the pan in one layer across the bottom. Place them in a large Dutch oven and add water to cover the pork by about an inch.

2. Place over high heat, let the water come to a boil, then reduce the heat to medium-high and place the lid partway over the pot so some steam escapes. Let it go at a strong simmer until there is only ½ inch (12 mm) of water left in the pot, which should take at least an hour and a half or up to a couple hours.

3. While the ribs simmer, that's the time to make the salsa macha: Heat the oil in a medium heavy-bottomed skillet over medium heat until it is shimmering but not smoking. Add the garlic cloves and fry, stirring, until they just begin to turn golden brown, about 2 minutes.

4. Add the chipotle and árbol chiles and the peanuts and fry, stirring, for a minute or two—the chipotle will begin to puff and the árbol will begin to get really dark brown, which is what you are wanting them to do. You just blister the shit out of it all. Depending on your chiles, you may actually smell them browning and burning more than see a major change in color. But either way, that's when you add the sesame seeds. Stir them in and let them continue to fry just until they begin to color—usually no more than a minute—then immediately remove the pan from the heat.

5. Carefully transfer the contents of the skillet into the jar of a heatproof blender, or if yours isn't heatproof,

transfer it to a heatproof bowl. (I've also used a food processor and I've used a mortar and pestle—it's a lot easier with something mechanical and powerful.) Let it cool until it stops sizzling. Everything will continue to darken and toast— that's OK.

6. Add a fat pinch of salt, the brown sugar, and vinegar to the oil and chiles. Blend until smooth, then pour into a container and let cool completely. Taste for salt and add more as needed. You'll have some salsa macha left over after you add it to the ribs, but it lasts forever in the fridge, in my opinion.

7. Check the ribs. The meat may be pulling away from the bones— that's OK. When the water is almost gone, remove the lid and reduce the heat slightly so things are just barely bubbling. What you are really waiting for is the water to almost totally evaporate and for the ribs to start to fry in the fat that's left in the pot. That's pretty much the concept here.

8. As the water begins to disappear, flip the ribs occasionally so they don't stick to the bottom. When they start to sizzle and brown in the fat, add ⅓ cup (70 ml) of the salsa macha, tossing the ribs with tongs so the salsa totally covers the ribs, and adding more as needed.

9. Remove the ribs to a platter or plates and serve with more salsa macha for dipping. Me? I would also serve these with a squeeze of fresh lime, a sprinkle of sea salt, a ripe avocado fanned out on a plate, and some hot white rice.

76.

MADRE DE SAGRANTINO

Montefalco, the city in Umbria, Italy, is magical. It's high up, with beautiful olive trees and grapes growing all over the place: It's just wine and olive oil all around. It's the home of Jean-Piero of Paolo Bea winery, an architect turned winemaker who is a godfather of natural wine, a winemaker's winemaker. Wine has been on his family's land forever—the sloped hills have two-hundred-year-old vines—and he grows Sagrantino grapes, originally from Montefalco. When I had lunch with Jean-Piero, he gave me one of the rarest things I have ever tasted—a jar of *madre de Sagrantino*, or "mother of Sagrantino," all the sediment left at the bottom of a thirty-year-old barrel of wine. The wine is up top, and the sediment slowly chills to the bottom and becomes gelatinous, this gorgeous natural wine jam from a barrel of Sagrantino from 19-fucking-89.

For lunch, his wife made eggs like my mother does: Start with a cold pan, then heat them up slowly so they have soft and delicious streaks of yellow and yolk. She put the eggs on toast made with some beautiful whole-grain harvest wheat with the sediment and the most virgin of olive oils. She also made a pasta, a tonnarelli with wheat grown in the area, and some clean summer vegetables, just perfect al dente zucchini and sugar snaps cut into very small pieces. Jean-Piero threw in more of that sediment and shaved ricotta salata over the top. Both were all the simplest of ingredients, but so mind-blowing. It was really the single most wild food experience of my life, because that madre de Sagrantino can't be re-created anywhere else: It's from one barrel of wine, aged for my lifetime. It's nuts, just to be the owner of a little of that.

In Italy, let me tell you, it's all about slow food and fast cars: This is what Modena chef Massimo Bottura (see next page) told me after I went to see him on that same trip. With everything, you have to take such special care, and you have to be very patient. Just to open a bottle of wine for the first time will take five years, as it's grown, made, aged, stored. To have a piece of cheese takes two years. In the States, most people don't ever really take the time to understand the time and process that goes into making those things, they just buy it and consume it without having any respect for the product. But in Italy, it's three, four hours to get lunch over with. It takes half an hour just to bring a bottle of water after you order it. Every person that I have met in Italy has the utmost respect for the product, for the ingredients, and it's still hard to get those back at home, even now. You can't get that exact cheese here, because it comes from thirty meters away, and you know the wine that went with it was from a guy in the middle of town that's making fucking incredible stuff.

Massimo, from Osteria Francescana in Modena, is the man: His psychedelic veal, his Five Ages of Parmigiano Reggiano, those are amazing. He reminds me of my producer Party Supplies, with the chaotic smart energy he has—I love that type of quality in a person. Here's a story to show you what type of dude he is. In Modena, after we taped a show at his restaurant, I needed sunglasses and I told him I was going to go walk around town and find some. It's the middle of the day, everyone in his kitchen is working, he'd just got number one restaurant in the world a few days before, and he decides he's going to get me a pair of sunglasses from his house. Because Persolé had just sent him like a hundred pairs of these beautiful custom frames, and what is he going to do with them all? He peels off in his black Maserati—and when I say peels, I mean peels—down those ancient Modena streets, comes back not ten minutes later, and finds me wandering around to give me the pair of sunglasses. I almost wonder if he had them in his car the whole time, just to fuck with me.

77

MY SPECIAL SAUCE

I learned to make My Special Sauce about a decade ago at this Frenchie-type place on Chrystie Street on the Lower East Side, where I worked for like two weeks. I was the *garde manger*, which meant I was the one making salads and sauces and cold dishes and other small little shit. The head chef was amazing—it was a Frenchie vegetarian type of place, whole ingredients and organic, right about when I first started hearing about organic. But the owner—I didn't like her and she didn't like me, and she fired me. Even so, I learned four things from that chef that I'll always keep with me. Number one is this herb and mayonnaise sauce, something he said he learned from his old head chef in Provence or some shit like that. He also made these chicken thighs where he cooked them skin-side down in a pan, letting them brown and brown and brown in their own fat, and then you eat those with this sauce. He taught me how to make real triple-fried fries, which also went with this sauce, and finally how to make cassoulet, which I also love.

MY SPECIAL SAUCE

Here we go, we're gonna zap.

MAKES 2½ CUPS (600 ML)

The actual making of the Special Sauce is fast and simple—you just zap it all in a blender—but it is phenomenal. These flavors are perfect together, which is why the Special Sauce is also now my universal sauce, meaning it goes on everything: chicken sandwiches, roast beets, smoked lamb, French fries, and the Purple Onion Rings that follow on page 190—that's the combination I used to serve as a bar special. I often use twice as many garlics—I love that burn. I will say that the French chef used Hellmann's, but when I first started making it I used Admiration, which is a little shittier, meaning it's the cheaper brand you get at the restaurant supply store. And for some reason, in this, it tasted better.

5 large cloves garlic, roughly chopped
2 cups (480 ml) mayonnaise
2 tablespoons drained capers in brine
1½ tablespoons caper brine
Juice of 1 medium lemon (2 to 3 tablespoons)
1 cup (32 g) loosely packed, roughly chopped parsley, tough stems removed
1 cup (24 g) loosely packed, roughly chopped dill, tough stems removed
Freshly ground black pepper

1. Combine the garlic, mayonnaise, capers, brine, and lemon juice in a blender or food processor. Zap to roughly blend.

2. Add the herbs to the bowl with the rest of the ingredients. Zap for a second or two.

3. Now add ludicrous amounts of black pepper and zap it all until it's all totally smooth and creamy, pausing occasionally to wipe down the sides of the bowl with a spatula so that you get it all in there. The end result should be somewhere between a dressing and a dip.

4. Taste for salt, adding more capers or caper brine if needed, or pepper or lemon juice, etc.

5. That's it. This will keep in the refrigerator for 4 to 5 days. Serve with Purple Onion Rings (page 190).

PURPLE ONION RINGS

(FOR DIPPING IN MY SPECIAL SAUCE)

Onions make you cry like a baby.

SERVES 6 TO 8

The best part about onion rings is you can pile them up when you serve them. I use red onions because they have a little more zip to them. You could dip the rings in a coat of flour first before you dunk them in the batter for a puffier, more tempura-like crust, but in my taste-testing the thinner rings are lighter and superior and stay crispy once they've started to cool off, like a kicked-up version of Funyuns. A rule of thumb: You can feed about two people with a really big onion.

2 cups (250 g) all-purpose flour
1–½ teaspoons salt
½ heaping teaspoon freshly ground black pepper
Tapatío or another red hot sauce
2–½ cups (600 ml) cold seltzer or sparkling water
2 quarts (2 L) vegetable oil
3 to 4 large purple onions, peeled
My Special Sauce (page 189), for saucing

1. Whisk together the flour, salt, and black pepper in a large bowl. Like the Special Sauce, this also has to be mad peppery. I just grind until the top looks like black snow.

2. Now hit it with about 3 tablespoons of hot sauce, then whisk in that seltzer. (You don't want to add flat water, because the bubbles make the batter airier and crispier.) Whisk until you have no lumps and it looks like a pancake-ish batter—when you move the whisk through the batter, you should see ribbons. Whisk in a little more hot sauce until the batter is a nice light pink, like the color of Russian dressing. You won't taste the heat so much, but the rings will fry up a nice golden brown.

3. Put the batter in the refrigerator for 15 minutes to let it settle a little bit, then line a baking sheet or a plate with paper towels.

4. Fill a Dutch oven or stockpot with the oil just a little more than halfway up the sides of the pot. Heat the oil over high heat until the oil begins to shimmer. It should be around 400°F (205°C) if you have a thermometer, but otherwise you can tell when it is ready because of the shimmer.

5. While the oil heats, cut the onions into ½-inch- (12-mm-) thick slices, making sure to separate the rings. It's better to make them a little bigger than a little smaller.

6. When the oil is hot, dip a few of the rings in the batter with tongs, flipping them once or twice so that they're fully covered. Shake off the excess and then add them to the hot oil just 2 to 3 at a time so they have lots of room to swim.

7. Flip them with a clean fork when they just begin to turn brown—this should only take a minute or two. Let them cook for another minute or two, until the other side is golden brown, then remove to the paper towels.

8. Repeat, adjusting the heat of your oil as necessary. Don't let it get too hot or too cool. But since you're only making a few at a time, you're good either way.

9. Serve these piled high with a side of Special Sauce. Obviously, the cook should keep the Special Sauce nearby the stove and just eat these as they're ready.

78

THE HOT SAUCE FROM 117

I've known Meyhem since junior high school and Body since I was seventeen. (Body's Albanian too, so we call each other cousins.) We would always go out to eat, find places to eat, and earlier on we would eat a lot at this one Puerto Rican restaurant at 116-20 Jamaica Avenue and 117th Street in Queens. We never called it by its name, would just call it 117, and the whole crew would always go there—Meyhem and Body and everyone I knew at the time. It would be the hangout, the meeting spot. They made this fucking hot sauce* that is one of the best hot sauces ever—chunky, tomatoey-orange, hot but amazing flavor. It's crazy good, and is totally unlike any other hot sauce anywhere else. It's now called Mi Casa Bar & Restaurant and is owned by Dominicans, but the sauce—it is still the same. Recently I went back, and one of the cooks finally told me what was in it: You take Clamato, garlic, hot sauce, cilantro, Cuban ají peppers, onion, celery, green bell pepper, and habanero salsa, and you liquidate all that in the blender.

✳ There is also the green sauce at Pio Pio, the Peruvian rotisserie chicken chain. It's like blended jalapeños with vinegar and garlic, though no one can really ever figure out what the fuck it is. It's banging. There are a bunch of them in New York City, though I always went to the original Pio Pio on Woodhaven Boulevard. ●

I feel like I also have to mention this Colombian street food festival that they do every weekend in the summertime in Flushing Meadows Corona Park in Queens. They dance and play soccer, they chill. There's people coming around selling you *aguardiente*. The cops just don't fuck with them, they let them party and drink, even though they are cooking on things that are not meant to be cooked on, like fencing that still has treatment on it. Whatever. They also have some of the best sauces that I have ever had, four or five different flavors of homemade *picante*, a yellow-green, a red one, some purple-looking shit. It's all some of the best shit I have ever had.

79. A FUCKING 270-POUND TUNA

At Shuko, a sushi place in Manhattan, chefs Nick Kim and Jimmy Lau broke down a 270-pound bluefin tuna from Spain for me and Jonah Hill to show us the parts nobody knows.

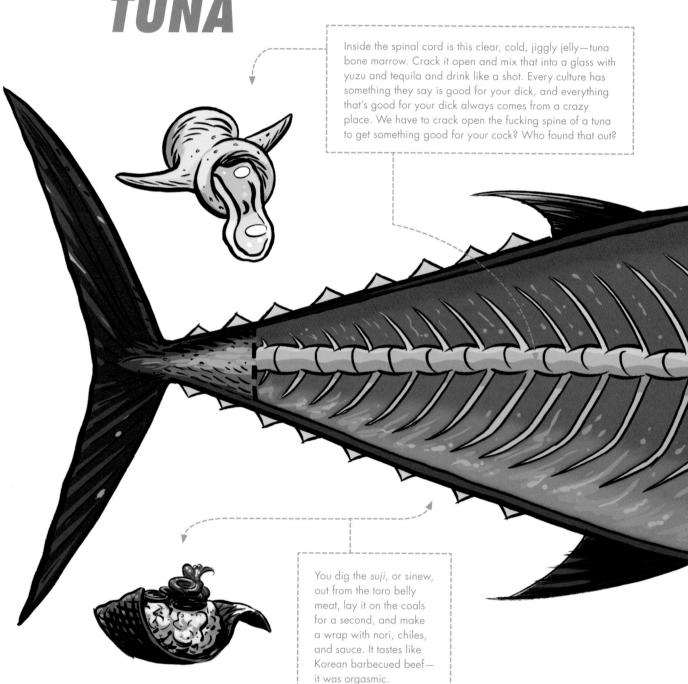

Inside the spinal cord is this clear, cold, jiggly jelly—tuna bone marrow. Crack it open and mix that into a glass with yuzu and tequila and drink like a shot. Every culture has something they say is good for your dick, and everything that's good for your dick always comes from a crazy place. We have to crack open the fucking spine of a tuna to get something good for your cock? Who found that out?

You dig the *suji*, or sinew, out from the toro belly meat, lay it on the coals for a second, and make a wrap with nori, chiles, and sauce. It tastes like Korean barbecued beef— it was orgasmic.

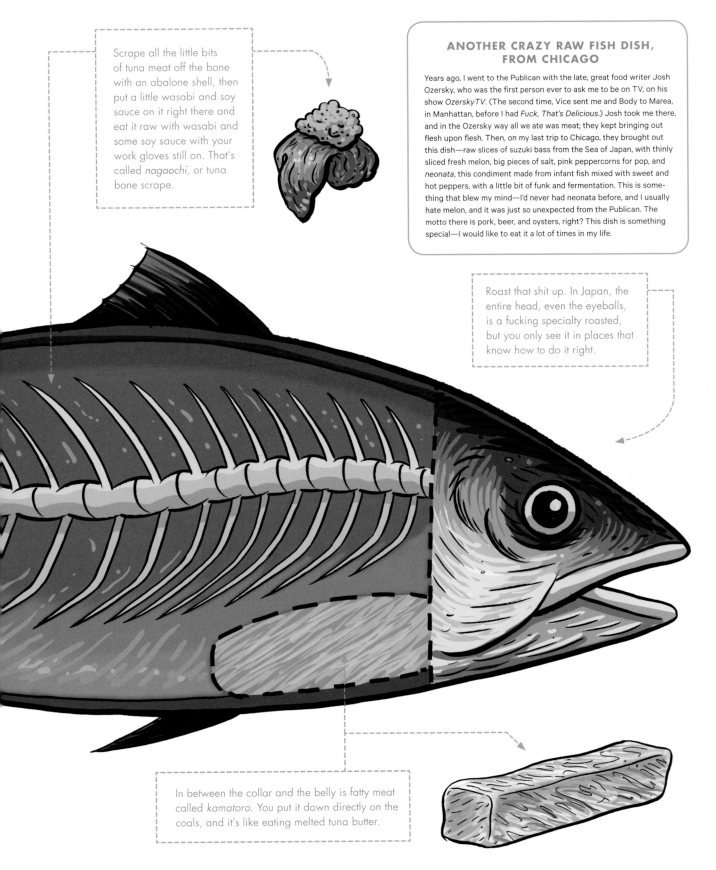

Scrape all the little bits of tuna meat off the bone with an abalone shell, then put a little wasabi and soy sauce on it right there and eat it raw with wasabi and some soy sauce with your work gloves still on. That's called *nagaochi*, or tuna bone scrape.

ANOTHER CRAZY RAW FISH DISH, FROM CHICAGO

Years ago, I went to the Publican with the late, great food writer Josh Ozersky, who was the first person ever to ask me to be on TV, on his show *OzerskyTV*. (The second time, Vice sent me and Body to Marea, in Manhattan, before I had *Fuck, That's Delicious*.) Josh took me there, and in the Ozersky way all we ate was meat; they kept bringing out flesh upon flesh. Then, on my last trip to Chicago, they brought out this dish—raw slices of suzuki bass from the Sea of Japan, with thinly sliced fresh melon, big pieces of salt, pink peppercorns for pop, and *neonata*, this condiment made from infant fish mixed with sweet and hot peppers, with a little bit of funk and fermentation. This is something that blew my mind—I'd never had neonata before, and I usually hate melon, and it was just so unexpected from the Publican. The motto there is pork, beer, and oysters, right? This dish is something special—I would like to eat it a lot of times in my life.

Roast that shit up. In Japan, the entire head, even the eyeballs, is a fucking specialty roasted, but you only see it in places that know how to do it right.

In between the collar and the belly is fatty meat called *kamatoro*. You put it down directly on the coals, and it's like eating melted tuna butter.

FRIED CHICKEN TEN DIFFERENT WAYS

80.
TOM YUM
At the Spicy Food Festival in Tokyo, I had one of the greatest things in the history of life that's ever been created: Bigger niblets of fried chicken tossed in thick Thai tom yum soup. It was lemongrassy, gingery, sour-y. It's fried, it's wet, it's ridiculous.

81.
MUSTARD-BRINED
I learned this somewhere along the crazy journey we call life: Use Gulden's or yellow mustard instead of a regular brine. It makes sense—there's vinegar in mustard, so it's just like brining it. Then you flour it, fry it, and it comes out oh-my-god-it's-so-fucking-crazy-good.

82.
TAIPAN HALAL DRUMS OF HEAVEN (2006-14)
Drums of heaven are fanned-out fried drummettes sauced with ginger, scallions, garlic, and chiles, and they were a big part of my life until Taipan changed up the recipe. It's Szechuan food by Bangladeshis—my mother put me onto it years ago.

83.
MAMAK SPICY MALAYSIAN

Immediately, no matter what, as soon as I get to Sydney, I go to this Malaysian restaurant Mamak. It has unbelievably spicy fried chicken with cinnamon and cloves—you already know there's going to be a line outside.

84.
THE ROY ROGERS WING

At Roy Rogers, where the fried chicken is awesome, they give you a wing with some of the breast meat still attached: That's my favorite piece of fried chicken, and they do the same thing at Popeyes Louisiana Kitchen. It's like an extra jewel.

85.
WILLIE MAE'S SCOTCH HOUSE

Fried chicken is a staple in an American household, and Willie Mae's in New Orleans is the quintessential American fried chicken. It's big pieces of chicken with a popcorn chicken crust, but it's not popcorn chicken.

88.
GOLDEN FOUNTAIN'S GOLDEN FINGERS

I feel like lemon chicken is a lost art, and this place in Queens is the master of the form. They deep-fry thick fingers of chicken in this puffy coat of batter and serve it with this thick lemon sauce on the side. (Also, the BBQ rib tips here are like burnt candy.)

89.
CHICKEN CUTLETS

My cutlet (see next page) is better than any cutlet in the world.* I have made a million of them, and I love them. They're really thin and just crunchy as hell. I used 4C Bread Crumbs back in the day, until Japanese panko arrived, and I fry them in olive oil.

* I did once have an incredible chicken *katsu* in Japan that I ordered out of a twenty-four-hour vending machine. You order from the machine and then pick it up from a window. It was two or three in the morning, I was by myself, fiending-out for weed, and in a bad mood and feeling down because I had just slept through the *fugu* meal—fugu is blowfish, which is poisonous if not prepared properly—everybody else had without me. I needed some comfort food, and I ate it right there on the crossing for the Shibuya Station on the stairs up to overpasses that help you cross over the street because the traffic is so bad. In the underpasses, there are homeless people with little house setups under the stairs, and they still take their shoes off before they go in the house, just like everybody else in Japan. ●

86.
CHICHARRÓN DE POLLO

I love Dominican fried chicken, which is fried little chunks of bone-in chicken with a thin crust and a touch of garlic and oregano. I like it with *yuca encebollada*, or the boiled yuca and onions from page 34.

87.
BONCHON CHICKEN

The chicken at this Korean chain is mad crispy-crunchy, plus the spicy one will really kill you with the spice. There's also a soy-garlic version, and you get those cubes of sweet, clean pickled daikon.

CHICKEN PARM

The perfect chicken Parm, made with the perfect chicken cutlet.

SERVES 2 TO 4

My favorite chicken Parm is the one I make myself with a cutlet pounded out just a little thinner than my usual. You want to add just enough of my Two-Minute Tomato Sauce (page 180) to coat, but not so much that you cover up the crisp of the chicken, and the cheese has to be oozy and bubbly and melted to a brown complexion. I prefer a platter over a sandwich, though you can get a decent one from your local pizza shop if you micromanage the experience. For either, there must be only one level of meat. If there are three levels of cutlet, the flavors are not in balance. This cutlet also has to be fried in extra virgin olive oil. Everyone is always asking: *I thought you can't fry in olive oil?* But you can, you just have to make sure it doesn't get too hot, because once it goes past that point, it's not amazing but disgusting.

6 eggs, beaten
8 ounces (226 g) panko bread crumbs
Extra virgin olive oil
2 large boneless chicken breasts
Two-Minute Tomato Sauce (see page 180), warm or at room temperature
16 ounces (450 g) Polly-O Whole Milk Mozzarella, thickly sliced

1. Put the eggs in one large baking dish and the panko in another.

2. Set a rack into a baking sheet and preheat your broiler.

3. Butterfly the chicken breast, open it up, and then pound it as thin as you can get it. This will take some time, and you should do it on a flat, large surface, as it'll get big. It will also become a crazy shape, like the entire country of Spain, but that's what you want.

4. Dip the chicken cutlets into the egg, then into the panko, punching them down hard so the panko kind of breaks a little, which will give you nice ridges for frying. Repeat, dipping the cutlet into the egg and then into the panko again, punching down hard and making sure the whole cutlet is covered with crumbs. Put them on a sheet pan and let them sit for 15 to 20 minutes to set up.

5. Fry the cutlets one at a time: Heat 1 inch (2.5 cm) of olive oil in your largest skillet over medium heat, but watch the oil to make sure it doesn't get too hot. Fry the cutlet on one side for 5 to 7 minutes or until the edges turn a dark golden brown—dark brown is OK, but you don't want to see black. As it cooks, use a spoon to baste the top with some of the sizzling olive oil. When the bottom has browned, carefully flip it over and brown the other side.

6. While the cutlet cooks, spread the bottom of a large ovenproof plate or baking sheet with a smear of the sauce. When the cutlet is done, place it on the sauce, then dollop on more sauce across the top, making sure plenty of the crispy edges of the cutlet are still exposed. Top the cutlet generously with slices of cheese, again making sure some of the crispy edges of the cutlet are still exposed. Repeat with the second cutlet.

7. When both cutlets are ready, broil them until the cheese is well-browned, bubbling, and even slightly charred in spots, at least 5 minutes.

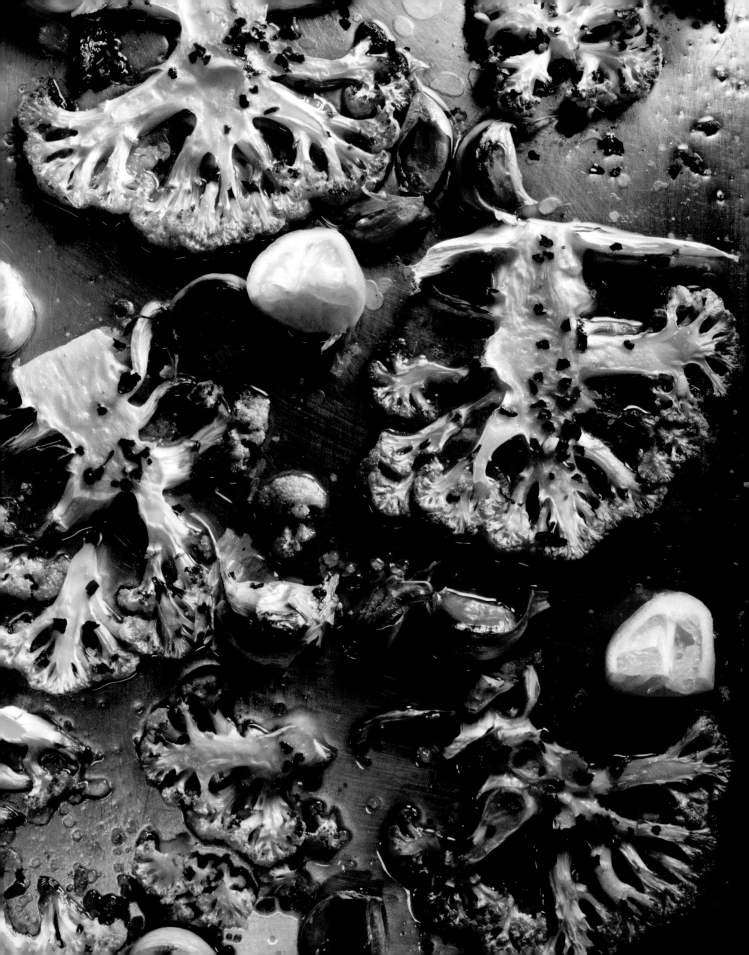

90

CAULIFLOWER

I love cauliflower, and I made it the morning Alchemist and I were recording the song "Big League Chew." As in, while it roasted in the oven with some olive oil, garlic, and chiles, we recorded the song. I used to cook all the time at his house in L.A., where he has his studio and where everyone hangs out all day long. I've made steaks, fried rice, ribs, and chicken on the grill. The first time me and ScHoolboy Q met, he walked in while I was cooking lamb—he tasted a piece, and ever since, we've been friends.

BIG LEAGUE CHEW CAULIFLOWER

For when I need something heart-healthy.

SERVES 4

This is such an easy dish to make—you only need a few ingredients: You've got extra virgin olive oil, which you should have in your pantry at all times; crushed red pepper, which you should have in your pantry; black pepper, which you should have; and garlic also needs to be chilling out in your crib at all times. Then you go out to the store and grab a fucking lemon. I mean, c'mon.

1 head cauliflower
⅓ cup (75 ml) extra virgin olive oil
Salt
½ to 1 teaspoon red chile flakes
Freshly ground black pepper
1 head garlic, separated into cloves
1 lemon

1. Preheat the oven to 400°F (205°C).

2. Cut the cauliflower crosswise into slices about ½-inch (12-mm) thick, then lay them out flat on a baking sheet. You want all those surfaces to touch the heat so the oil gets everything nice and crispy.

3. Add on all the little extras that fell off when you sliced it in between the slices, and do it so they fit nicely—gotta make that shit look beautiful. Drizzle the oil evenly over all the pieces. It's really easier to just drizzle it on from the bottle instead of measuring—be generous with it, but don't let the slices swim.

4. Use your fingers to sprinkle the cauliflower lightly with salt and the chile flakes, then the pepper—just grind it all over. Sprinkle the unpeeled cloves evenly over the pan.

5. Let it roast for 45 minutes to 1 hour, or until the bottoms are well-browned and the edges are slightly crispy. (Check it at 30 to make sure the pan isn't dry—if it is, add a drizzle more of oil.) Slice the lemon in half and squeeze it over the pan and sprinkle with a little more salt. Eat straight from the pan, squeezing out the soft garlic from the cloves onto the cauliflower with your fingers.

91. ALASKAN WHALE BLUBBER (A HELL OF A THING)

The first and only time I've been to Alaska, the second day we were there we were supposed to take a seaplane to go fly-fishing for trout, which I've always wanted to do. I'm actually an outdoorsy type of guy—I would have loved that. Just flying in, I got to see all the crazy landscape up close and in person for myself. It looks like one of those paintings hanging in a lodge or something, where you see the huge snowcapped mountains and the fucking ice and then just total green. But my stomach hadn't been feeling right, so I sat it out while my two boys Alchemist and Meyhem went ahead. Back at the house, I'm smoking, I am drinking black coffee—and I never drink coffee—all trying to make myself shit because I thought that was the thing to do. But after about four hours of torturous pain, at three in the morning, I got scared and went to the emergency room. They did a CAT scan, and they had to do an emergency procedure right away for entangled intestines—I'd had hernia surgery a couple of years before. I had to immediately cancel whatever else I was going to do in Alaska and go to a clinic to recuperate for almost a week before they sent me home, telling me I was all good.*

---

* I flew private on the way home, blasting Jay Z's *Reasonable Doubt*. On a private plane, you can lay on the ground, you can get naked, you can do a handstand, and a twelve-hour flight takes only six hours. You pay for the time, but it's worth it: Hey, I'm not six years old anymore—I don't fit in coach.

So the one thing I actually got to do in Alaska was go over to an Inuit's house, where she had gathered some younger kids who explained to me all the native Alaskan traditions their families have carried on for years and years. But then, this lady starts pulling out the indigenous meats. This was actually the first day of the trip, and even though I already felt sick, I went to her house anyway—because you can't go all the way to Alaska and not see anything. So there I was, my stomach hurting while she is pulling out frozen cubes of caribou and seal oil. The beluga whale blubber and the bowhead whale blubber, the seal meat and the black meat, which is meat preserved in the seal oil. So that's actually what I had been doing the day I went to the hospital, posting pictures of it all on Instagram. Later, Andrew Zimmern hit me up by direct message and said something like: *Man. That fucking whale blubber is a hell of a thing. I ate too much seal oil and they had to throw me in the snow—my temperature went up to 103 in ten minutes.* It was because of the density and richness of the fat—that's what fucked him up. And it is next level. But, of course, for me, it was the hernia.

Bebidas

92.

Virgin Piña Coladas

I don't remember the first time I ordered a virgin piña colada, but I do remember the last time. It was in the Loews Santa Monica Beach Hotel right off the pier with the Ferris wheel—one of the places I usually stay when I am working in Los Angeles. I would get one of these on my way back up to the room every night. The bartenders would always look at me like I was crazy, so I would tip them an extra ten bucks. I ran a bar for years—so I remember what it's like for them. The characters who always came in every day, they get a name. One guy's name was Beefeater Joe, because he always got a gin—he had a red face and always wore a golf pullover—and then there was Irish Kevin, who drank Jameson. I am the Virgin Piña Colada Guy, and I always ask for extra maraschino cherries.

93. Strawberry Mint Lemonade

Just blend this, and it's fucking sick: Ice, fresh strawberries, lemon sorbet, honey, mint, and freshly squeezed lemon juice.

94.
Chocolate Abuelita

Chocolate Abuelita (say it like I do: *Cho-ko-lah-tay Ah-bwel-lee-tah*) is spiced hot chocolate with cinnamon and other things, like the way it would have been drunk back in the day in Mexico. The Mexicans who worked in kitchens with me showed me Chocolate Abuelita—we would go out and get it at the C-Town supermarket and then drink it out of the glass mugs from the restaurant's bar. It is a big pie-shaped slab of chocolate that you break into Trivial Pursuit–shaped wedges and stir into boiling milk until it's frothy, traditionally with a wooden whisk-like thing called a *batidor* or *molinillo*. We drank so much it was almost a problem. *Abuelita* means "little grandmother," and Abuelita, she is almost one hundred years old and now owned by Nestlé, but I can tell you that in my humble dealings with all the Mexicans I ever worked with, they prefer her to Ibarra, which is the other brand you can easily find in the United States.

95. MORIR SOÑANDO

This drink is mad Dominican. I say *morir soñando* to a Dominican—it means "die dreaming"—and they go *ohhhh!* They just light the fuck up, like I mentioned Michael Jackson. The one that I get all the time is from Kissena Townhouse Diner near my mother's house—it used to be called the Dominican Diner Restaurant, and we had the number written on the wall by the phone. It's pretty much orange juice, sugar, milk, and ice, but you can make it with the cheap orange juice or with the fresh-squeezed, which I prefer, though with that one you have to really keep stirring it as you make it. Some people make it with milk and sugar, some people make it with sweetened condensed milk, or with evaporated milk and sugar. I really like it all ways, as long as it's banging.

This goes perfectly with a fat blunt.

SERVES 4

I usually make my morir soñando with a touch of vanilla and sweetened condensed milk—you don't need to add sugar, and it comes out more like an Indian mango *lassi*. I actually used sweetened condensed coconut milk for Wendy Williams when I made this for her show, which was amazing. I wanted to make it with *mofongo*—this crazy Dominican dish with crispy mashed fried plantains and gravy that all New Yorkers know—because I wanted to change mofongo's life forever and have hipsters eating it everywhere. But Wendy doesn't eat meat, so I made tuna poke and morir soñando instead.

Ice
2 cups (480 ml) orange juice
1 cup (240 ml) sweetened condensed milk
1 to 2 drops vanilla extract

1. Fill a pitcher with ice.

2. Pour the orange juice and then the condensed milk and vanilla over the ice, then stir it all aggressively until it is mixed.

3. Serve immediately, making sure some of the ice cubes are in each glass.

Snapple Lemon Tea

When I was in high school, I was addicted to Snapple Lemon Tea—I would drink twelve of them a day, seriously. It has this crisp, clean taste that is good with everything. I prefer it from the glass bottle, which must be kept freezing cold for best results, and then you have to shake the shit out of it and then slam the bottom of the bottle with the palm of your hand, so the top pops. You know how people like packing a new pack of cigarettes before they peel off the cellophane? It's like that—it's just a dance you do to extend the amusement. Back then I got them for eighty-five cents each from the Key Food supermarket across the street from my mom's house. I have since weaned myself away from sweet drinks—today I usually just drink water—but I still love a Snapple.

Crystal Light

A big part of my youth—
they put something in there
that's addictive. ●

98. FOCACCIA WITH AUSTRALIAN FETA AND SATSUMAS

Fetahhh.

SERVES 2

Feta cheese is a big thing in my life.* I love all types: The salty and creamy French, dense Greek, Bulgarian, which is the one that was always in my house, and most recently the spreadable marinated Australian kind from Meredith Dairy, which is a mixture of sheep and goat's milk and is incredible with that garlic and thyme inside the oil that they soak it in. This recipe is a new thing I have been doing, simple but amazing. It works best with the very best focaccia you can find.

1 small square loaf focaccia
Extra virgin olive oil
8 ounces (225 g) olive oil–marinated feta,
    at room temperature
1 pound (450 g) satsuma oranges, peeled
Calabrian chile oil

1. Preheat the broiler.

2. Cut the focaccia into slices 1 inch (2.5 cm) thick, then brush them liberally on all sides with olive oil.

3. Toast the bread slices on one side, then turn and toast the other. (I like to get all four sides.)

4. Spread the feta on the toasts. Pile them on a serving tray in a nice fashion, then place the oranges on the tray and drizzle everything with Calabrian chile oil. Eat both, one after the other.

* One of the best roast chickens that I have ever had is the one from Souvla, this Greek spot in San Francisco, where it's brined in the salty water that their feta cheese comes in.

99. KNOWLEDGE OF THE ANCIENTS

Foraging is dope. It's like fishing, hunting, and whatever else you do to go get the food on your own—it's that primal connection with the earth. This kind of knowledge has been lost, because there's no one to pass it down. Who's passing down foraging knowledge to me right now? My father's an immigrant from Kosovo, my mother was born in Brooklyn: We don't have the knowledge of the ancients. I wish I did, which is why when I was in Perth—on the western coast of Australia, far as a motherfucker, hot as a motherfucker—I met with this dude whom everyone calls Yoda. Yoda is a special chef who runs a company called Forever Food, where he forages and then cooks it all out in the elements—a little like the experience I had with Sazi the Ital in Jamaica on page 118. Yoda trained under the foraging dudes at Noma in Copenhagen, and he also learned under Australian aborigines. He uses all of Western Australia as his kitchen, and the food that he is finding and cooking, people have been eating for fifty thousand years. He took us to the beach, and so pretty much everywhere that we were there was food: These little lobster-type deals called *marron* smoked over coastal rosemary, dune spinach, finger limes, and pigface, one of the most incredible things on this earth.

It's like a little rosebud that grows on the ground at the beach and it tastes like a salty fig. Then we jumped into the shark-infested* Indian Ocean—it's the most incredible color turquoise you've ever seen—to dive for razor fish, this long shell hiding a little corn kernel–size nugget of soft meat. It had the texture of a clam and the sweetness of a scallop.

It is very satisfying to be able to go into nature and just grab something and make something incredible with it, which is why I should also talk about Ben Shewry in Melbourne. Chef cooked me the most elegant dishes I have ever tasted in the kitchen at his place Attica, which has a huge garden that we walked through together. A little tamale of very gentle whitefish wrapped in tree bark and smoked over embers, served with lemon myrtle butter and oyster meat, finger lime, and cress. This amazing apple dessert that takes seven people to make, an egg foo yong he made up with Danny Bowien from Mission Chinese that had chop suey greens from his garden. That was one of my favorite kitchens that I've ever visited. He's somebody that all my buddies in the food game talk about—that he's a G. I got the chance to finally meet him, and lo and behold, he was the G that was bespoken of him.

✱ A lot of people are scared of sharks, but I felt like if I got killed by a shark it would be an honor—after all, we're in their area. So far I've seen a dorsal fin, but I've never come face-to-face with a shark. I have come face-to-face with a bear, in the Poconos at a trailer park called Eagle Lake with my family. I went to go throw the garbage out, and there were a lot of older Albanian women there, so everyone leaves their shoes by the door. I put on the closest shoes to the door to throw the garbage out, and it was my aunt's little heels, these little slippers. So I am opening the door and this fucking bear comes out and he is like, *Argghh.* And I just threw the garbage and took off running in those heels. In the Poconos, in heels, running from a bear. It was hilarious.

100. WONTONS

When I was a youth, my mother had a friend named Helen Choy, who owned a Chinese restaurant across the street from my house with her husband, Joe. They made everything themselves—they were ill. That's where I was introduced to Chinese food and where I became a wonton eater for life. Wontons are up there with the bagel for me. Helen would always give me some of their wonton soup whenever I came in, because I loved their wontons so much. Often the flavor of the meat in a wonton just tastes off, but at Helen's, everything was harmonious. In the wonton soup, she gave you all those nice pieces of roasted pork, though I would often get the whole plastic tub filled with just wontons. My mother would always get the combination soup with the shrimp and roast pork and noodles and all that other shit in it, but I would always eat the wontons out of it. (I also like putting those crispy noodles of fried wonton skin into the soup and letting them reconstitute, while leaving a little to the side to have crunch on top. Those are banging when you let them reconstitute. It's like another fucking beast.) It was hearty dumplings at Helen's—I also like those very delicate ones, those silky ones from the nicer Chinese restaurants that are kind of like homemade ravioli, very gentle, though those creeped me out at first. Helen and my mother also had a Korean friend named Theresa, and both Helen and Theresa had sons who went to school with me. The six of us became good friends, and Helen and Theresa would take us out to eat in Chinatown and in the Chinese and Korean parts of Flushing in Queens. They knew all the good places. Eventually Helen and her husband sold their place and it became New China Garden, where I would order the chicken and broccoli and Dutches from page 44.

INDEX

My dog Coco is from Colombia, so he only speaks Spanish. He's eighteen, though I feel like he must be ninety in human years. He has lost an eye and he won't eat anything but real food. In Colombia, he once ran away for a month. They found him four towns over chilling with the local street dogs. He had a bandana and a tattoo that said *Thug Life*.

PHOTOGRAPHER
GABRIELE STABILE

PHOTOGRAPHER
FOR FTD/VICE
JACK NEWTON

ADDITIONAL
PHOTOGRAPHY
TOM GOULD

DESIGNER
WALTER GREEN

EDITOR: Holly Dolce
PRODUCTION MANAGER: Anet Sirna-
 Bruder
CREATIVE DIRECTOR: John Gall
MANAGING EDITOR: Gabriel Levinson

PHOTOGRAPHY ASSISTANT: Jon
 Santiago
FOOD STYLIST: Rupa Bhattacharya
FOOD STYLIST ASSISTANT: Jenna Liut
PROP STYLIST: Nidia Cueva

FROM VICE + MUNCHIES: Chris
Grosso, Justin Cymbol, Sean Stewart,
Lauren Cynamon, Elana Shulman,
Peter, Bernardo Garcia, Barry Frish,
Farideh Sadeghin, and John Martin

ADDITIONAL SUPPORT: Leda
Scheintaub, Amelie Cherlin, Patty
Gloeckler, Anna Wahrman, Sarah
Massey, Michael Sand, Jennifer Brunn,
Paul Colarusso, Mary O'Mara, Danielle
Young, Eddie Barerra, Marc De Jesus,
and Marc Gerald

Special thanks to Mario Batali for the
Foreword

Library of Congress Control Number:
2016960983

ISBN: 978-1-4197-2655-2

ABRAMS The Art of Books
115 West 18th Street, New York, NY 10011
abramsbooks.com

ILLUSTRATOR
JOHNNY SAMPSON